SECOND LIVES

Becoming a

Freelance
Writer

Also by Bill Harris

Second Lives: Becoming a Consultant
Second Lives: Becoming a Desktop Publisher

SECOND LIVES

Becoming a
Freelance
Writer

Bill Harris

Introduction by Charles L. Sodikoff, Ph.D.

St. Martin's Griffin ✖ New York

Library of Congress Cataloging-in-Publication Data

Harris, Bill, 1933–
    Second lives : becoming a freelance writer / Bill Harris.
        p.   cm.
    ISBN 0-312-20004-8
    1. Journalism—Authorship—Vocational guidance.   2. Freelance journalism—Vocational guidance.   3. Feature writing—Vocational guidance.   I. Title.
    PN151.H418   1999
    808'.06607—dc21   99-15141
                                                                                                    CIP

First St. Martin's Griffin Edition: August 1999

10 9 8 7 6 5 4 3 2 1

Contents

808.066
HAR
258-4129

INTRODUCTION

Starting over? What does that mean to you? To some it means opportunity, challenge, and growth. To others it means danger and defeat. To everyone it means *change*.

Change is defining the course of America today. Millions of us who have spent the first part of our working lives employed by someone else are now—either unwillingly or by our own initiative—starting over. The options are clear: find another job in your current trade, find a job in a new trade, retire (if you can afford it), or work for yourself.

Second Lives is a guidebook for those who are considering using the experience and skills acquired working for someone else to go into business for themselves.

Going into business is like learning to ride a bike. Remember that first try? Someone held the bike and ran alongside. You pumped your legs as hard as you could, wobbling wildly as you tried to keep the front wheel straight. Then suddenly you were on your own, but you probably didn't get very far. Maybe you scraped your knees when you fell.

After that there were some more bumpy rides, falls and scrapes but eventually the ride smoothed out and a whole new world opened up. Our lives changed. We had more independence. We traveled to new places and did new things. We kept up with some of our friends and left others in the dust.

That's exactly what starting a new business is like.

Second Lives is the guiding hand on the back of your bicycle. It will help you make the decision as to whether or not to go off on your own; identify the type of business you ought to pursue; and give you the support to launch your business successfully.

Starting you own business may be the most exciting, but hair-raising adventure you ever take. I know, not only because I have counseled many people who have tried it, but also because I have done it myself. At age forty-eight, I decided to open my own consulting practice after years and years of working for someone else. The trip has been exhilarating and my second life has been the happiest of my entire career. Sure, there have been scary periods and times when I wasn't so certain I would succeed, but with a strong motivation, the proper skills, and the flexibility to adapt to the ever-changing needs of my business, I am well on my way.

I hope this book helps you make the right decision for yourself. If you do choose to go out on your own, put on your helmet and be prepared for the most exciting ride of your life.

—*Charles L. Sodikoff, Ph.D.*

SECOND LIVES

Becoming a
Freelance
Writer

CHAPTER ONE

A World of Your Own

At one time or another, just about everyone has had a dream of being self-employed. That may be your dream right now, and if the job description that goes with it is "freelance writer," there has never been a better time to declare your independence. Not only has the computer revolution produced new opportunities for writers—from websites to newsletters to specialized magazines—but the Internet has made it possible for you to find markets for your work thousands of miles away with clients you may never meet face to face. More and more freelance writers today are submitting their work by E-mail and doing much of their research online as well. Their independence now extends beyond avoiding the nine-to-five grind to the option of getting out of town and resettling wherever the spirit moves them.

The decision of whether or not to go off on your own will take a great deal of soul searching. There's no denying that starting your own business takes a lot of courage. You'll be facing a host of road blocks in your path, one of the biggest of which may be the fear of change.

Most people find change frightening, but you might be surprised to discover that change really isn't unfamiliar territory. Chances are you're not doing your job in the same way as you did five or ten years ago, and you've been dealing with change for longer than you might think. Back in your father's day, holding a job for twenty or thirty years often added up to one year's experience twenty or thirty times. But experience is something quite different in today's world. You may be surprised to find that change is already a big part of your life.

Another key consideration is the question of security. There are no guaranteed weekly paychecks or health benefits when you work for yourself, but keep in mind that security also has a new meaning today. Not too many years ago, people expected to retire from the same job they started out in whether they liked it or not. But companies have changed, and so have people. Attitudes also have undergone change. Nobody expects a job to last a lifetime anymore.

The silver lining in all this is that we're freer than we've ever been to try something new and change our lives. There may never have been a better time to put yourself in control of your own destiny.

YOU'RE NOT ALONE

Most freelance writers don't think of themselves as operators of small businesses because by definition they work alone. But even if it is a lonely business, it will be your way of supporting yourself, and it will be up to you to produce enough income to make ends meet. No matter how you define it, when you go off on your own you're going to be in business for yourself just as surely as if you were opening a boutique or starting up a restaurant.

Being in charge of your own life is at the heart of the American dream. It's the same promise that brought our ancestors here; it's what built the country, and it's what still drives millions of Americans. According to a 1997 survey by the Entrepreneurial Research Consortium, as many as 4 percent of American adults are in the process of starting up more than three million small

> I had seven different bosses in two years—not much stability there. So I went to work for myself. After a few months, my mother asked me why I wasn't looking for a job. I told her I didn't have time because I was too busy.
>
> —Lisa Kirazian, Los Angeles, CA

businesses. The survey also revealed that one out of every three U.S. households—thirty-five million of them—includes someone who at one time or another has followed the dream of going into business for him or herself. It's happening all around you. Old people, young people, men and women, are walking away from unsatisfying nine-to-five jobs, time-wasting commutes, office politics, and unappreciative bosses.

Many of us have known them—bosses who were either unfair, unyielding, incompetent, insensitive, mean-spirited, double-dealing, or all of the above. That's no fun, and one of the reasons why you may have bought this book is because you don't want to spend the rest of your life working for people who sometimes seem to go out of their way to make life difficult.

Going into business for yourself gives you a chance to use the skills you've developed working for someone else to create a whole new life—only this time around it can be tailored specifically for you, with more freedom, interest, and satisfaction.

IT'S YOUR LIFE

Of course, it's pretty easy to talk yourself into staying put. You might be telling yourself that striking out on your own isn't a realistic thing to do. But consider one of the joyous realities of modern life: we're all probably going to live to see our seventy-fifth birthday, and most likely quite a few after that. Do you really want the second half of your life to be a carbon copy of the first?

> I always wanted to freelance, then one day I told myself, "Do it or quit talking about it." Now I can't stop talking about how glad I am that I did it.
>
> —Laurie Mendoza, San Francisco, CA

You may be short-changing yourself if you don't explore what's out there. These days there are so many different options and opportunities—especially for writers who have quickly become a cornerstone of this "information age" that is changing the world.

Consider what's happening in corporate America. Downsizing leaves hundreds out of work; Wall Street cheers and the victims have anxiety attacks. The gurus of big business preach that getting rid of deadwood cuts a company's costs, the survivors work a bit harder, and stock prices go up. But there is only so much work a company can squeeze from its people, and its commitment to stay lean and mean usually means it can't hire new employees either.

These days, it's considered good business for companies to "go outside" and hire independent contractors to get the work done. By and large, that represents a huge opportunity for freelance writers because whatever else management thinks it can do without, the business world still turns on the written word. Even companies that have grown rather than downsized are using more outside help than ever before. It's a very good time to declare yourself an outsider.

FOLLOW YOUR DREAM

At some point in their lives, everybody has dreamed of making it big. Some do, and some just make it better. The first step is to get rid of the illusion that you need to play out the hand you've been dealt. It's never too late to wipe the slate clean and take

> When I was working and found the same assignments coming around for the seventh and eighth time, I began to lose my enthusiasm. I found it again by striking out on my own.
> —Beth Friedman, Austin, TX

charge of your life. It's *your* life, after all, and there is no reason why it ought to be unsatisfying. If you think your own ideas are better, don't waste them on the suggestion box. Use them for yourself. You never know where they'll take you—until you try.

> People I knew were being downsized and I decided to jump before I was pushed. I figured that if I had to depend on somebody for a paycheck, it might as well be me. I haven't had a slow week since, and I'm making double what I made back then.
> —Mark Herman, Jacksonville, FL

CHAPTER TWO

What Is a Freelance Writer and How Do I Become One?

"In pleasanter days, I had amused myself with writing letters to the chief paper of the territory . . . and had always been surprised when they appeared in print," he said. Then a letter arrived from the paper offering him a salary to become its city editor. It wasn't a lot of money, but to him "it looked like a bloated luxury—a fortune—a sinful and lavish waste of money." He recalled, "When I thought of my inexperience and consequent unfitness for the position, my long array of failures rose up before me. Yet if I refused this place, I must presently become dependent on somebody for my bread. . . . So I was scared into being a city editor. I do not doubt if, at that time, had I been offered a salary to translate the Talmud from the original Hebrew I would have accepted . . . and thrown as much variety into it as I could for the money."

The reluctant city editor was Mark Twain. Needless to say, the job he described in *Roughing It* didn't last very long, but it gave him a new career. By his own account, until that job came along, "I had gained a livelihood in various vocations, but had not dazzled anybody with my successes."

He may never have been asked to translate the Talmud, but

the rest of his life was filled with as much variety as anyone could wish for. He's remembered today for his successes as an author, but his contemporaries were dazzled by the things he wrote for magazines and newspapers as a freelance writer, and he might be among the first to say that he was something more than just an author.

AN OLD TRADITION

Like Mark Twain, a great many well-known authors have hired out their pens to enhance their cash flow. These freelancers, writing for hire, one job at a time, have been finding satisfaction, and a comfortable lifestyle, for centuries. In the last century, they were called "scriveners," and before that they were known by the more genteel name "scribes."

As the name has changed, so have the media and with them the opportunities. But the basic thing that supported those scriveners still applies: even in societies where most people know how to write, not many of them know how to put words together so that other people can understand what they are trying to say. This is the job of a freelance writer.

A CORNUCOPIA

Down through the ages, hundreds of well-known books, autobiographies, and other works attributed to what we call "celebrity authors" have been turned out by anonymous ghost-writers, one of the more lucrative aspects of the freelance trade. Assignments, such as ghost-writing books or speeches and reports for executives and others who need their thoughts translated into simple English, is just a small part of the world of opportunities open to freelance writers. Related to this field is a whole specialized area known as technical writing, which, simply put, is rendering esoteric information into an accessible form. This would include fact sheets for doctors who prescribe a new drug, a user manual for computer software, or even the instructions for assembling that bicycle you just bought.

If you've been looking at classified ads, surely you've seen by now job solicitations for "grant writers." These are usually placed by arts and educational organizations whose lifeblood is the grants they receive from philanthropic foundations. While some of those organizations have grant writers on their staffs, many more hire freelancers to do the job. In the business world, companies frequently hire outside writers with similar skills to edit and rewrite the proposals they submit to prospective clients explaining plans for a project or a new service.

In some ways, freelance writers who specialize in grant writing or business proposals are close professional cousins to promotion copywriters who write ads and brochures, direct-mail pieces, and other marketing tools for all kinds of businesses. Both are paid well for writing that sells—whether it's convincing a consumer to buy a product, a company to buy a service, or a foundation to fund an idea.

Financial writers often write promotional copy as well. Banks, insurance companies, and other financial institutions are constantly creating new services, and it usually falls to a freelance writer to explain them in language their customers will understand. Some of those same writers also make a specialty of providing the words that explain the numbers in quarterly and annual reports.

Public relations writing, which runs the gamut from speeches to press releases, is yet another form of selling with words. The goal of good PR writing is presenting facts in a way that puts a client's best foot forward and attracts the right kind of attention. In many ways, public relations and promotional writing require the same basic skills, and many writers have examples of both in their portfolios. However, in public relations, getting the facts straight is critical and it thus is closely related to journalism.

Writing magazine articles comes under the heading of journalism and has become one of the fastest-growing ways for freelancers to support themselves. Computer graphics programs have lowered the production costs of magazines and have made a whole new field of niche publishing possible, and just about every new magazine opens up a fresh market, and subject, for freelance writers.

An even newer area of opportunity, and one that is growing by leaps and bounds, is writing websites. Until quite recently, the words that popped up on the World Wide Web were usually written by the computer hackers who created the sites themselves. By now, however, most of them have conceded that their talents are better suited to hypertalk than plain English, and freelance writers have jumped into the breech. It is not only making the Web more useful and more interesting, but it adds another dimension to the world of freelance writing.

THE LITERARY LIFE

Before the advertising community began calling a copywriter's output "the creative," it was usually known as "literature." It sounded good, but nobody was really fooled. More often than not—when the writer wasn't within earshot, of course—the effort was also called "boilerplate." But the writers weren't fooled, either, and just as journalists have traditionally dreamed of writing the Great American Novel, most writers working in other fields also yearn to become authors and create real literature.

But for every six-figure advance on a novel, the number of rejection letters sent out by publishers reaches into the six figures, too. Still, it's a dream worth following, as long as you keep your day job—or, better yet, become a freelance writer.

Writing is like exercise—you have to work at it every day. But you also have to eat every day, and make sure there is a roof over your head. Freelance writers with literary goals can have it all—a steady income, a variety of writing assignments, and time to listen to their muse. In fact, having different kinds of writing jobs is probably the best antidote to writer's block there is. And having an income can make the difference between a struggling author and a productive one.

There was, however, a well-publicized 1995 National Writer's Union survey of 1,143 of its members that revealed that the median income of its freelance writers came to an appalling four thousand dollars a year, but there may be a couple of factors at work that can make the number deceiving. For one thing, many writers freelance part-time, and income like that can add up to a terrific sideline. For another, the NWU's membership dues are based on one's income from writing. Under five thousand dollars a year it comes to ninety dollars, and over twenty-five thousand dollars the fee more than doubles. It may be possible that some of the union's members low-balled their income reports. In any event, you shouldn't let the survey discourage you. With the right skills and effort, believe me, you can do better.

HOW MUCH CAN YOU MAKE?

The NWU's own guide to freelance rates reports that writing copy—advertising, reports, brochures, and other collateral material—for commercial clients ranges from thirty to seventy-five dollars an hour, and only slightly less for technical writing. For articles in trade publications, the rate per word ranges from fifty cents to one dollar, and for consumer magazines the rate is typically double that. The union also says that the usual advance for a nonfiction hardcover trade book ranges between ten and fifty thousand dollars.

Although the rates it quotes are averages, and the NWU strongly recommends asking for higher amounts, it's fairly clear that just about any writer can easily make many times the median income the survey said they earn.

DO YOU HAVE WHAT IT TAKES?

The creative process is a mysterious thing, but there are ways to measure it. The Human Engineering Laboratory of the Johnson O'Connor Research Foundation has been doing it since 1922. Every set of tests it gives at fourteen locations around the country is compared to more than 300,000 other tests and the career paths of people who have taken them. The results provide insight on a person's aptitudes for a myriad of things, including writing and editing.

It is possible that you have already been writing for someone else, and at this point you're contemplating going off on your own. Or perhaps you are a newcomer to the field, but believe you have a knack for writing. Either way, it isn't likely that taking an aptitude test is among the things you were planning to do before becoming a freelance writer. You probably already know what your professional strengths are, and your weaknesses, too, but some of the things the Foundation has discovered about what it takes to be a successful writer might help you understand how those strengths and weaknesses can make a difference.

Among the areas it explores is what the testers label "graphoria," which is the ability to check things quickly and accurately. This is measured by the timed regrouping of columns of numbers. It is a skill every editor needs, and according to the research, it turns out that women are as much as 75 percent more likely to have an aptitude for it than men who have taken the test.

The ability to come up with new ideas is usually considered a writer's stock-in-trade, but they've found that successful journalists don't seem to have a lot of talent for it, probably because their job is not inventing facts but reporting them. The researchers at Johnson O'Connor have found that people who have a strong aptitude for this thing they label "ideaphoria" are likely to change jobs a lot because they need more creative challenge than any single job can give them. If that has been your experience, and you consider yourself a strong idea person, you'll probably take to freelance writing like a duck to water.

The patterns the tests have revealed suggests that one of the keys to success in freelance writing is the ability to concentrate on long-range goals. Another desirable quality, called inductive reasoning, is the ability to see relationships in what ordinarily appear to be unrelated ideas and information. The researchers have noted that people who score low in this area usually have an accepting nature and a lot of patience and do well in the corporate world. High scorers, on the other hand, have instincts that make them good critics, and they do well, not only as writers but in just about any profession.

It goes without saying that a large vocabulary is basic to any writer's chances for success. But after all these years of testing, Johnson O'Connor has found that the highest vocabulary scores are racked up by business executives. Writers come in third, after editors. The tests have also revealed something else: while a high vocabulary doesn't guarantee success in any field, a low one almost always leads to failure.

But when all these things are weighed in the balance, the testers say that knowing your aptitudes is only part of your blueprint for the future. One of the tests Johnson O'Connor gives measures personality, and separates "objective" traits from "subjective" ones. Everybody's makeup comes from one or the other, they say, but never a combination of the two. Their research finds that three out of four people have objective personalities—that is, their outlook on life takes a broad view. They are more likely to react to problems with an external view rather than through inner thoughts or feelings. If you are in that category, and also have an aptitude for ideas, chances are you'll do well in advertising and marketing.

Subjective people are more likely to look at life from a personal point of view, and an overwhelming majority of writers fit that mold. They are more likely to be individualists, with an ability to focus on a single problem for as long as it takes to work it out. They actually prefer working alone and it annoys them to have anyone else involved in their work.

If you have a subjective personality, it may be what is drawing you to freelance writing in the first place, but beware: subjective people don't often have much patience with other people's points of view about their work—neither editors nor clients nor even their spouses. Even though it may help to have that kind of personality in a business that requires you to work alone, you'll need to be able to swallow your pride and accept the inevitable outside opinions. Otherwise, you're going to be very lonely indeed.

A NEW LIFE

You know that you have the aptitudes to become a writer and the personality to make it a happy choice, but what if the kind of work you're currently doing involves little more than writing memos, letters, and reports?

The Johnson O'Connor researchers say that unused aptitudes are what's at the root of most career crises. If you've been making use of some, but not all, of your abilities through your working life, they believe, the abilities you've neglected will at some point assert themselves and you'll find your outlook changing. For instance, if writing is among your aptitudes but you've built a career around your ability as a manager, chances are you'll eventually find management unfulfilling. That's when you may begin to think about writing a novel or a screenplay and your old career will begin to pale by comparison. This is the time you may consider a second career as a freelance writer.

Having said that, the next question is, How do you go about doing it? Terms like "hard work," "tenacity," and "determination" come to mind. But ask a writer what it takes and the word you'll hear most often is "luck"—not the kind of luck that helps you win the lottery, but the kind that comes from recognizing opportunities when they come along and then doing something about them. It's the kind of luck you make for yourself; it's a game anybody can win.

CREATING YOUR OWN WORLD

Joni Prittie started her freelance career as an artist, but one day she came up with an idea for a gardening book and, just for the fun of it, she put it in the form of a proposal to a San Francisco publisher. "I had never written anything more than long letters to friends," she recalls, "and I hyperventilated and fell off my chair when I found that the proposal was accepted and I had to come up with 35,000 words. It was a stroke of luck, but I didn't know what to do with it until a friend said, 'Joni, you *talk* 35,000 words every time you drive up to the city.' So I simply 'talked' to my computer and turned out that first manuscript." It wasn't her last. Far from it. She still sells illustration and design, but her main business after thirty years as a freelancer is her writing, and she couldn't be happier about it.

Sandy Jones, who has been a freelance writer for twenty-five years, began her working life in social services, but she found the job depressing, and to get away from it, she settled for a job selling china in a department store. Leaning heavily on a the-saurus to find fancy words to string together, Sandy had been the star feature writer on her college newspaper. The applause of her professors gave her the confidence to try writing for a living, and to get some experience, she volunteered her services to the department store's advertising department. She got more than experience. The advertising manager taught her more about writing in a couple of months than a whole university-full of professors could in four years.

"She taught me the most important lesson I've ever learned,"

Sandy says. "She showed me how to speak out loud." It worked wonders in creating advertising copy, but the concept is working just as well in her career as an author of books and articles on parenting and child care. Her readers couldn't be more delighted, and she hasn't opened a thesaurus in years.

Although most writers learned the basics of structure and technique at school, a large number of them have also gone through apprenticeships in low-level jobs. The lucky ones, like Sandy Jones, have found mentors who have shown them how to translate theory into practical applications.

Sometimes writers discover their talents almost by accident. Karen Gravelle is one of them. Although she has been a successful technical writer for years, she is quick to tell you that writing "wasn't my idea." When she earned her Ph.D. in biopsychology in the early eighties, she envisioned a lifelong career studying the behavior of lizards; but grant money was hard to come by, so she answered a classified ad offering a job as a medical writer. The work involved writing reports on cancer immunology, a natural lead-in to the AIDS research that was just beginning to emerge at the time. Eventually she quit her job and jumped into this new field. "I love technical stuff, and can understand what scientists are talking about," Karen says, "and I find it easy to distill the information. We all learned together, and I became an expert in the field." Although she's in demand as a technical writer, Karen has another life as an author of books for teenagers on animals and anthropology. She smiles conspiratorially when she explains, "It's a hobby that pays for itself. I love to travel and to study other cultures. A book I did on Native Americans, for instance, allowed me to live on a reservation for a couple of months, and the advance paid all my expenses."

Pete Witcher started out in Minneapolis selling slot machines to Indian casinos until he became an office manager for a small mail-order catalog company. The company was so small that everybody on the staff, Pete included, contributed copy for the catalogs. Until then, it was a talent he never realized he had. Before he left for a full-time writing job, he was not only writing entire catalogs but all of the company's correspondence as well. When he struck out on his own as a freelance writer, "jumped into it" as he puts it, his specialty was as a technical writer producing software manuals.

INDEPENDENT CONTRACTORS

Some magazine publishers encourage freelance writers whose work impresses them to sign on as independent contractors working exclusively for them. It can seem like a marvelous arrangement with desk space in the publisher's office and a guarantee of steady work, not to mention the visibility among editors who might one day offer you a staff job. Whether such an arrangement works or not depends on your personality, your motivation, and your desires.

When you change your status from freelancer to "independent contractor," there is more than just semantics involved. Yes, you'll probably get more assignments, but the rate of pay probably won't change and you'll still be responsible for your own taxes. On that score, you'll lose your deduction for your home office as well as most of the other expenses you could declare as a freelancer. You'll also lose the freedom to sell your work to other publishers. And although you show up for work in the publisher's office, you'll have none of the advantages associated with staff work—no health benefits, no sick days, no vacation time. You may even, as a "visitor," have to pay higher prices at the company cafeteria. The word "independent" in these arrangements more often than not doesn't fit the writer as closely as it does the publisher. You will find yourself tied to them, but they will consider themselves independent of you.

Yet some writers find this to be a good deal. It gives them the prestige of working for a recognized and respected company and still allows them to keep some of the freedom associated with being on their own. They don't have to follow a strict schedule as long as they meet their deadlines, and they are free to take days off and long vacations on their own without begging for approval. And, generally, these independent contractors are able to turn down assignments they aren't comfortable with—as long as they don't make a habit of it.

It often happens that writers go for arrangements like these because they can lead to permanent jobs. If this is your ultimate motivation, you'll have to consider the offer if your publisher suggests that you should sign on as an independent contractor.

In the early 1990s, the Internal Revenue Service began telling big companies with on-site independent contractors that these people were actually "common-law employees," and that millions in taxes was long overdue. The companies responded with a definition of their own, and began calling them "temps," which created a bonanza for temporary agencies. But the jury is still out, literally, as a case against Microsoft on its use of temporary help grinds its way toward the Supreme Court.

In the meantime, think twice if your definition of "freelance writer" doesn't quite square with an editor's proposition to come aboard and trade some of your freedom for a little security. It may not be as good as it seems.

THE SPICE OF LIFE

Freelance writers who are doing the same things they did when they were working for a steady paycheck are rare. Even those who picked up where they left off when they decided to be their own boss have discovered new interests. It goes with the territory. When you are a freelance writer, no experience you've ever had is wasted, no interest needs to be unfulfilled. The key word is variety. Every assignment is a learning opportunity, and every-thing you learn represents a chance to do something new. Can you think of any other way to have as much fun? And . . . earn a living while you're at it.

CHAPTER THREE

A Day in the Life of a Freelance Writer

The prospect of not having a boss interrupting your train of thought every five minutes may be one of the reasons why you're hoping to be your own boss one day, but don't think there won't be interruptions you didn't plan for, and days without enough hours to get everything done. No more than there is a typical freelance writer, is there a "typical" day when you become one, except that most of them will be long and many will be hectic.

When you begin working for yourself, your routine will best be determined by your own rhythms. Some people find they work best late at night, others believe they do their best work at the crack of dawn. Either way, you won't be living in a nine-to-five world anymore, and although you'll need to be bright-eyed and bushy-tailed for contact with your clients during their regular business day, you will be free to write at times when you feel most productive.

However, that doesn't mean you can put off writing until you "feel like it." Self-discipline is the key to success in running any small business, and for a writer it is crucial. Set up a routine for yourself and try not to vary from it unless it is unavoidable. The nature of the job will get you all the variety you could wish for, and will help prevent your routine from becoming mundane.

A few of the freelance writers interviewed for this book agreed to describe a day selected at random, in their own way and in their own words. The days they chose may not be typical of their working lives, nor of yours when you go into business for yourself, but together, they'll give you some clues about what might lie ahead.

DEBRA JASON—Boulder, CO

Debra is a freelance advertising writer who specializes in direct marketing and produces brochures. She also writes for websites, although she does not develop them.

I got into my office at 8:30 this morning, although 9 is my usual time (I don't work at home). My routine is usually to check my voice mail and then my E-mail. Since I'm already online, I answer the E-mail messages first and then respond to any voice mail I may have. If something develops as a result of these messages—it could be a copy revision, a request for a fax, E-mailing a file—I deal with it before I go to the coffee shop downstairs for a café au lait.

Then I go to my datebook, where I'll have listed (the night before) what I need to get done today. Usually, the list starts with projects I've been working on, then phone calls that need to be made, letters to write or samples to send out. I'll turn to the project with the highest priority and begin working on it.

At this point, I'm on the computer writing, but I'll answer the phone when it rings, and continue on with the project until I'm either finished or saturated. It's rare that I take lunch, but usually nibble on something while I'm working.

Yesterday I spent a lot of time proofing a website for a client whose business is mortgages, and wrote copy for a newsletter for the Cherry Creek Shopping Center in Denver. I also worked on my own newsletter, "The Copy Cat," which I send to clients and prospects every quarter, featuring marketing articles and tidbits of information.

I left the office at about 4 to go to a Business Expo sponsored by the Denver Metro Chamber of Commerce. There, I schmoozed with other professionals, networked with colleagues and made some new acquaintances.

JIM MCCLURE—La Grange, IL

After twenty-eight years in corporate public relations, Jim took a buyout and went into business for himself. He specializes in writing news releases, sales training manuals, and seminars as well as product literature for the telecommunications industry.

I occasionally put on a necktie and venture forth to meet with clients, but the vast majority of my days are spent in jeans working in my home office. Even though working at home is highly flexible, I make it a point to be at or near my desk during the regular business hours my clients observe.

Most days I am at my desk by 9 A.M. (unless a client calls earlier) checking my E-mail and downloading any newswire items captured by America Online or CompuServe. My Macintosh is programmed to turn itself on at 5 A.M. to receive any faxes that come in. I do some writing during the day, particularly if I'm on deadline. However, much of my day is spent researching—tracking down subject matter experts, playing voice-mail tag, and interviewing. I also use my daytime office hours for keeping in touch with my clients, networking with other professionals and, when time permits, contacting prospective new clients. Whenever I can, I consume the *Wall Street Journal* and CNN during my lunch break. One luxury of working at home is that I am usually able to get to the health club by 5 unless I get a better offer from a client.

I usually wind up putting in a couple of hours after supper, interspersed with surfing the 'net, watching TV and otherwise goofing off. Sometimes this is the best time to focus on a writing project without interruptions or to make the final push to meet a client's deadline. I welcome (and get) a lot of quick-turnaround projects because the flexibility of my work-at-home style equips me to meet unreasonable deadlines on "mission impossible" projects. Clients are delighted when my finished work is waiting for them via E-mail or fax first thing in the morning.

ELIZABETH JUDD—Washington, D.C.
Elizabeth, who among other things is a business writer, works as a freelance book reviewer for clients such as *Publishers Weekly, Microsoft Sidewalks,* and *Salon.*

7:30– 9 A.M. Read the remaining 50 pages of *The Antelope Wife* by Louise Erdrich so I could begin reviewing it for *Salon.* Deadline's today.

9–11 A.M. Wrote a first draft of the Erdrich review.

11–11:30 A.M. Made calls. Tried to set up an interview with Howard Amer at the Federal Reserve for an upcoming profile for *E-Money.* Called Mike Castle's press secretary for clarification on a question in a completed *E-Money* piece.

11:30 A.M.–NOON. Handled E-mail. Realized I couldn't download files for a work-family information booklet for a new client, Ceridian Partners. E-mailed them about the problem, and followed up on a fax I hadn't received. Sent an E-mail to *IR* magazine letting them know that I'd only have time to accept one of the two articles they proposed for the June issue.

12–1:30 P.M. Researched background on Grace Paley on the Internet and wrote two paragraphs on her upcoming D.C. appearance for Microsoft's *Washington Sidewalk.*

1:30–2:30 P.M. Rewrote draft of the Erdrich review.

2:30–3:45 P.M. Had lunch in the park with a friend.

3:45–4:30 P.M. Returned phone calls I'd missed. Talked with editor on the Ceridian project and scheduled a conference call for the next day.

4:30–6 P.M. Doctor's appointment.

6–6:30 P.M. Re-edited my Erdrich review.

HOLLY ADAMS—Denver, CO

Elizabeth is a technical writer who works on multimedia training manuals, CD-ROMs, and scripting for companies like Hewlett-Packard and Lucent Technologies. Some of her assignments are team efforts, where each writer is responsible for a particular segment of the job.

I woke up this morning at around 8, had coffee and read the paper (this part is ritual). The phone rang a few times, but I let the machine pick it up and take messages. I spent the next hour returning phone calls, sending E-mails and compiling material I need to submit to a writing contest.

The following few hours I consulted with two teammates on a current technical writing project and sent each of them electronic samples of our prototype. I discussed the possible parameters of a video script and accompanying workbook with a new client, and I revised two columns for submission to Microsoft's *Denver Sidewalk* website.

By noon, I had submitted the articles by E-mail, heard by telephone and E-mail from another teammate, debated taking a shower and decided to postpone it. Had another conversation with a potential new client. Then I gave an interview to another writer, returned more phone calls and E-mail. I spoke with an insurance rep about changing my health insurance, prepared a résumé to send to a company that asked for it last week, and consulted with one of my mentors about preparing a bid for the potential new client.

At 2, I ate a bagel and then spent the afternoon sifting through content material for the current project and separating out what I will be using for development. I tasked out the potential new client, priced the job and faxed out a bid. Now it was time for a shower and sushi with a friend.

I returned home at about 10 P.M., picked up E-mail and responded to a current project manager's concerned message. After sorting through some more content for the current project, I began sending out my last batch of E-mail for the day at about 12:30 A.M.

Most days I work later into the night. One of the reasons why freelancing works so well for me is that I am like a vampire. I work best when it's dark outside.

CARL NELSON—Monkton, MD

Carl says, "I make nearly all my money writing advertising: ads, brochures, radio and TV spots, training and sales videos and whatnot." In his spare time, he is putting the finishing touches on his second novel.

Let me tell you about this week, which has been rather busy for me. On Friday, I was in Florida on a location shoot for two TV spots I had written earlier. On Saturday, I edited them. On Monday, I wrote an ad for a financial company in D.C. inviting visits to their booth at an upcoming convention. The next day I wrote a full-page ad for a boat manufacturer. Not counting a free trip to Florida, I made $2,400 this week, which is nearly all net since I work at home with virtually no overhead. If I spent $2,000 a year on business supplies and expenses, I'd be amazed. Somebody lock me up. This has to be illegal!

LISA KIRAZIAN—Los Angeles, CA

Lisa is a grant writer who gave up a staff job to freelance for a variety of arts organizations. She also writes articles, newsletters, and annual reports for nonprofits. With the time she has left over, she polishes her screenplay.

I usually wake up at 9 A.M. or earlier, and read the *L.A. Times* from cover to cover over breakfast. Start work at 10. I begin with checking E-mail, faxes and making/returning phone calls. If that day is a deadline day, I usually start off by finishing the deadline project to get it out as early in the day as possible. Then I make calls. I usually work on calls/deadlines until around noon, then I work on some of *my* stuff—my scripts, marketing and personal calls—and then I check my E-mail again. Then I work on upcoming projects not due right away, but soon—grants, reports, articles. I work pretty steadily until 3 in the afternoon, when I read the day's U.S. mail and break for lunch. Around 4, I go out and do errands related to the work I've done that day—photocopying, FedEx, post office—so that I can make the 5 o'clock deadlines. When I come back, I check my E-mail again and return a few last calls or faxes until about 6, when it's time to close up shop and make dinner.

That was an example of a "in-office" day. I try to schedule "meeting" and "in-office" days so that when I go out I can get a few meetings done at once, and then my days in the office can be uninterrupted. I usually schedule meetings for mid-morning or right after lunch to avoid rush-hour traffic.

BETH D'ADDONO—Philadelphia, PA

Beth was a feature writer on a local newspaper before starting her own business. She writes books, magazine, and newspaper articles on food, entertainment, and travel. She also does some business and public relations writing.

I put in regular and long hours in my office. Of course, I travel also, but I typically work from 8:30 until 6. Then I'm out in the evening for reviews and so forth. One recent typical day began with phone calls to set up a food story in Atlantic City. Then I wrote a travel column for the Gannett paper and a music column for the *Daily Times*. I answered E-mail, interviewed a chef, fielded phone calls from angst-ridden musicians wanting me to write about them, and pestered PR people to make sure I got the release, the cookbook, the invitations. I arranged for slides to be sent for next week's travel column—opened mail—did a "Yes, I got a check!" dance—filed some of the mail. Then I took my dogs for a walk and when I got back sent off a memo to the editor with three ideas for next month's magazine story. (My brain sometimes feels too picked by editors, by the way. Do I have to do their job for them or what?)

CLAY MORGAN—Memphis, TN

Clay began his writing career when he sold his first magazine article at age fifteen. He still writes for magazines, but his business has expanded over the years to include public relations and promotional writing for small businesses. He also operates a judo school.

I get up at about 7 A.M. and stumble—literally, because the cats almost always trip me up—to the office. I fire up the computer and check/respond to various E-mail messages. I get a quick shower, spend a little time with my cats, get a glass of juice and get back to it. It's about 8:15 by now.

First on the agenda is writing a press release for a client. That takes a little better than an hour. I'll zip it to the client for approval via E-mail when I log back on after lunch. I spend the rest of the morning concentrating on an article I've been working on. It's one of those that seemed real interesting at first but is sort of bogged down. I've got to find a way to fire it up.

While working on the article, a friend calls. He's a world-class athlete in judo, and he was asked to submit two pages on himself for a book that's coming out. He says he doesn't like writing about himself and asks if I'll do it. Naturally, I agree. He says a fax is on the way—articles and stuff that has been written about him that I can use as research. *Thirty-nine pages* later the fax is done. The project isn't due for a couple of weeks—on the back burner it goes.

After lunch, I concentrate at first on mundane projects—respond to a couple of letters, send out some requests for magazine guidelines and sample issues. I also write a query letter and mail out letters to five ad agencies, introducing myself and my services.

I check the mail—yuk! No acceptance letters and no check, although my bank was kind enough to send me a credit card bill. I decide to call a lawyer about that missing check, but change my mind. Ten minutes later, the client is receiving a nasty fax, along with my fifth and final invoice. I make up my mind to definitely call a lawyer if I don't have the check in a week.

I log back on and send the press release I wrote this morning. I spend a little too long goofing around the Internet. When I finally log off, it is past 3:30. The next hour is spent proofreading an annual report. Then I spend the rest of my writing day working on my novel. Not much progress today—oh well.

AND THEY WOULDN'T TRADE IT FOR ANYTHING

If the approach to their average working day varies according to their output and their personality, there is one thing every successful freelance writer agrees about: they wouldn't trade their life for anything else. As Debra Jason puts it, "My daily routine may seem boring to some people, but I'm not bored by what I do. Having my own business as a freelance copywriter is the first time in my life I can truly say I love my job."

CHAPTER FOUR

Thinking It Through

Clay Morgan, a Memphis-based writer, started his freelance writing career when he was fifteen years old. Clay had been a high school national judo champion and when he sold the story of his young life to *Martial Arts Training* magazine, he knew that he had found a career. He has been writing magazine articles ever since, and has built a solid business doing public relations and promotion writing as well. He's never worked for anyone else but himself.

Kimberly Rufer-Bach of Boulder Creek, California, was seventeen when she sold her first article. She had written it for her high school newspaper but the editor refused to run it. She took it to a local weekly newspaper and not only got it published, but got paid for it, too. She's been contributing articles to the paper ever since. Kimberly's first love is editing, and that, along with ghostwriting, is at the heart of the business she has built for herself since the day her story didn't make it into the high school paper.

Are Clay and Kimberly typical freelance writers? They are in terms of the businesses they've built for themselves, but not in the way they started them. Most freelance writers use the work experience they've gained employed by someone else to create a new business of their own.

When Jim McClure, a public relations and technical writer in La Grange, Illinois, was downsized out of a telecommunications company he knew that his twenty-eight years of experience was valuable. Although Jim's buyout was generous, he was too young to start collecting retirement benefits. But he wasn't ready to retire anyway. He was having too much fun as a writer, and he knew his experience as a technical writer in a fast-changing field would be in demand. In fact, his biggest client welcomed him with open arms. It was, by the way, a subsidiary of the company that had shown him the door. Fortunately, he hadn't closed it behind him.

The decision to go from the security of a regular job to the uncertainty of striking out on your own should begin with an honest look at what you have to offer. Analyze your strengths, your weaknesses, your past experience, and your talents. Take a personal inventory of what works for you and what doesn't, and think about what you expect from the future.

Working as a freelance writer requires an enormous amount of self-discipline. You'll need to be able to deal with deadlines and to push yourself to keep on working whether you like it or not. And you'll also have to be able to deal with loneliness. One of the most frequently cited reasons people give for wanting to go into business for themselves is the opportunity to "be on my own." Freelance writers are much more than that. Their work is done in what amounts to solitary confinement. The local librarian will in comparison look like a social butterfly.

You're going to be on your own, making a living through your talents without a guaranteed paycheck, health benefits, and security. More often than not, you'll deliver a job and be out of work until you find the next one. Like everything else, freelance writing has its downside, but as long as you're prepared, the roadblocks you run into won't necessarily be problems you can't overcome.

EXPLORE THE MARKET

No matter how they arrived at the decision to become freelance writers, by and large most never seem to have given a second thought to "the competition." Many say that they don't have competitors, only "colleagues," and, in some ways, that's a reflection on the nature of the business.

If you were setting up a car dealership or opening a restaurant, it's undeniable that you'd need to make sure you have a competitive edge before you start, but writing is a very personal business, and no matter how many other people are available in your area with the same specialty, none of them will write in the same way. The business of freelance writing is much more closely related to custom cabinetmaking or designing sailboats than selling cars or running a restaurant. But even cabinetmakers and sailboat designers need to look around them before they begin selling their services. They need to know where their markets will be, who else is in that market, and how difficult it will be to become established.

PLAN FOR SUCCESS

Debra Jason had worked for several New York advertising agencies before she decided to become a freelance writer. She had gone to college in Colorado and was eager to relocate there, so she went to Denver on a vacation and while she was there she contacted every ad agency in the local phone book. The answer in nearly every case was "we're downsizing," which Debra saw as an opportunity. It was obvious to her that those agencies were going to have to hire freelancers to get the work done. Most of the laid-off copywriters she talked with said they weren't planning to freelance, especially for the people who had given them pink slips. Many of them were heading out of the area in pursuit of greener pastures. She figured she was in the right place at the right time, and in a few weeks she was back to stay. That was ten years ago, and Debra has one of the most successful freelance writing businesses in Boulder today.

Some freelance writers don't think it's important to start out with a business plan, even one as simple as Debra's. You may have a gut feeling that you can make a success of freelance writing, and since it doesn't take a lot of money to get started, it may seem easier to just go ahead and wing it. Of course you can. It just isn't a good idea.

It's possible that you can make it as a freelance writer on just talent alone, but if you hope to be secure doing it, you need to think of freelance writing as a business as much as it is a fulfilling career. Keep in mind that once you're on your own, fulfillment will also mean supporting yourself.

ASK THE EXPERTS

As a writer, one of the personality traits you may have developed is independence. It's an important one that every successful writer shares. But no matter how independent you may think you are, you'll never be completely free of the rules and regulations that affect every small business, even if you're not aware of them.

What is it worth for you to know about the things that could rise up to haunt you after you start your business? How does free expert advice sound to you? Right now, just around the corner and waiting for your call is a retired business executive who wants to share the experiences of a lifetime with you.

An agency of the Small Business Administration called the Service Corps of Retired Executives (SCORE for short) specializes in helping people like you who want to be on their own. These volunteers can tell you just about everything you need to know about starting up a new business and keeping it alive. One of them will know exactly how to put together a business plan, and how local, state, and federal laws will affect your new venture. And, the consultation won't cost you a dime.

You'll find the nearest SCORE office listed under "U.S. Government" in the phone book along with the numbers for the Small Business Administration. You'll also find the agency on the Internet under the keyword SBA. All of its services are free, and they're all designed to help you make your business work.

SCORE has more than three hundred offices across the country, staffed by more than thirteen thousand volunteers, all of whom are seasoned business veterans. It isn't very likely you'll find a former freelance writer among them—most freelance writers would never dream of retiring—but there are basic rules that apply to every small business, and SCORE's volunteers are on hand every day to show you how those rules can affect yours.

Yes, you're a creative person, and you may find financial details difficult if not boring, but it goes without saying that when you're in business for yourself, keeping a close eye on your finances is a matter of life and death. The people at SCORE will help you simplify the financial aspects of your business, not just at the beginning but down the road as well. In terms of your initial start-up investment, most of the rules that apply to other small businesses probably won't apply because as a freelance writer you can get up and running on a shoestring budget. Still, there is an investment required even if it is a small one. You may need computer hardware and software, for instance, as well as office supplies and the furnishing of the office itself.

Most accountants, and probably the people at SCORE as well, will advise you to have as much in savings as it will take you to live for six months or a year. It's solid advice and you should take it. But you'd be surprised how many freelance writers don't. Lisa Kirazian, a freelance grant writer in Los Angeles, admits she's among them. "I spend money too fast," she says, "and I just concentrate on making it as I go along." Her attitude is a reflection of one of the personality traits most writers share, confidence in themselves. It may be an admirable quality, and another key to success, but wouldn't you really rather not have to worry about money when you're juggling words in the air? And wouldn't it be great to be able turn down jobs you'd rather not bother with?

IS THIS BUSINESS RIGHT FOR YOU?

Making a success of your freelance writing business has less to do with your personality, or even your writing style, than with your attitude. You may think of yourself as an entrepreneurial type, and that can surely be an asset when you go into business for yourself. But things like self-discipline and organization, attention to detail, dealing with people, and occasionally doing things you may not enjoy are what will determine your success.

Try the following questionnaire written by Charles L. Sodikoff, Ph.D., a psychologist and career management professional who has counseled people like you for the last fifteen years. It will add to your understanding of whether you have the ability and willingness to go off on your own.

PROFILE FOR SUCCESS

Take a minute to circle the numbers that apply to you:

Ability to Do
4 = Real strength
3 = Able to do
2 = Need to work on
1 = Real weakness

Willingness to Do
4 = Really like doing
3 = Not a problem
2 = Do not want to do
1 = Will not do

	Ability to Do	Willingness to Do
Managing your own time	4 3 2 1	4 3 2 1
Organizing your day	4 3 2 1	4 3 2 1
Working long hours	4 3 2 1	4 3 2 1

	Ability to Do	**Willingess to Do**
Working on weekends	4 3 2 1	4 3 2 1
Putting personal and family plans on hold	4 3 2 1	4 3 2 1
Meeting people/talking to strangers	4 3 2 1	4 3 2 1
Mixing business and social activities	4 3 2 1	4 3 2 1
Selling yourself to others	4 3 2 1	4 3 2 1
Selling your services	4 3 2 1	4 3 2 1
Working with demanding or difficult clients or editors	4 3 2 1	4 3 2 1
Respecting other peoples' opinion of your work	4 3 2 1	4 3 2 1
Changing your work even when you think it is perfect	4 3 2 1	4 3 2 1
Initiating new projects	4 3 2 1	4 3 2 1
Working on your own without having others to share ideas	4 3 2 1	4 3 2 1
Setting long-range goals and specific targets	4 3 2 1	4 3 2 1
Taking a planned and organized approach to work	4 3 2 1	4 3 2 1
Juggling multiple jobs at one time	4 3 2 1	4 3 2 1
Doing clerical tasks	4 3 2 1	4 3 2 1
Working under tight deadlines	4 3 2 1	4 3 2 1
Looking for creative solutions to problems	4 3 2 1	4 3 2 1

	Ability to Do	Willingess to Do
Making difficult decisions	4 3 2 1	4 3 2 1
Solving problems on the spot	4 3 2 1	4 3 2 1
Dealing with uncertainty	4 3 2 1	4 3 2 1
Having patience to "stick-with-it" through slow periods	4 3 2 1	4 3 2 1
Investing your own money	4 3 2 1	4 3 2 1
Understanding and maintaining financial records	4 3 2 1	4 3 2 1

SCORING

ABILITY TO DO

If you gave yourself scores of "1" or "2" on three or more items, you need to carefully examine how these things are going to get done when you are in business for yourself. First determine how important they are for the specific type of writing you plan to do. If you are writing advertising copy, for instance, you may never be asked to make a difficult decision; or if you write magazine articles, you'll probably have your expenses paid; but if you have a low score on an item that appears to be essential, are you going to be able to acquire the ability?

WILLINGNESS TO DO

If you gave yourself scores of "1" or "2" on three or more items in this column, then you need to carefully examine your level of commitment to your new business. Examine each problem area and determine how likely it is that this will be required in your new life. If these are things you know must get done, and you aren't going to be willing to do them, then you must ask yourself if freelance writing is really for you.

BE HONEST WITH YOURSELF

You may be able to fool all of the people some of the time, and some of the people all of the time, but the one person you can never fool is yourself. Of course, you are eager to have your own business, but when you are making plans to go out on your own, be sure you do it with your eyes wide open. It's your life, and the only way to be sure of success is to be honest with yourself before you start down the road.

CHAPTER FIVE

Defining Your Business

"One of these days, I think I might drive up there to meet him." Monty Montgomery was talking about the editor of the magazine he's been writing articles for since the mid-1950s. The editor is in Michigan; Monty is in Hondo, Texas. They've never met face-to-face.

Although he started his freelance writing business before the Internet was established, using the telephone and overnight shippers, he has served clients as far away as Europe. Today, Monty routinely uses the Web to find assignments and to deliver completed jobs. He even used it to find an artist to illustrate a monthly magazine column he writes. He's never met her, either.

In most businesses, geography is destiny. You wouldn't expect to become a tycoon selling air conditioners in Northern Maine or heating systems in Southern California. A family drugstore across the road from a shopping mall is probably doomed to failure as would be a Hard Rock Café in a retirement village, but thanks to the World Wide Web, most freelance writers are in control of their own destiny, and are able to run their businesses from anywhere in the world.

The opportunities are wider than the Web, in fact. Traditional wisdom may say that if you want to write for advertising agencies, your chances will be better if you live in a big media center such as New York or Chicago, but when New Yorker Debra Jason set out to become a freelance advertising copywriter, she turned her back on Madison Avenue and took her portfolio to Colorado. Sandy Jones finished her apprenticeship in a big-city department store, then went home to Brevard, North Carolina, to start her new career as an author and authority on child care.

What each of these writers have in common, apart from living in unexpected places, is that they have each developed a niche. And the world, it seems, is beating a path to their doors.

Finding a niche is indispensable *before* you start your business. Without it, you have no realistic way of finding the work you need to get a solid start. Of course, your business will evolve over time and your specialization may change, but it will never get off the ground to start with unless you know exactly what the core of your new business will be.

Jessica Freedman left her job as a legislative director on Capitol Hill to work with her sister on an Internet advice column, "The Advice Sisters." "We're the Siskel and Ebert of dating," she says. They came up with the idea by scouting bookstores to see what was selling and concluded that "everyone wants love." They also concluded that "most of what was out there was garbage," and immediately set out to correct the situation. They have already published two books on the subject, and although they may find another area of interest one day, they have built a solid niche for themselves. Jessica believes that "it is imperative to find your niche and be persistent about it. It is a slow process, but a worthwhile one."

LET YOUR NICHE EVOLVE

Jessica's jump from the world of law and politics into the hearts of people looking for help was the result of careful research into the market, and by the time she and her sister landed on the

Internet they were off to a running start. But as she doesn't mind telling you, it is possible that they will find a new niche and might change their direction for the long run. It's an experience most successful freelance writers share. Although many create niches for themselves as experts in one field or another, as Karen Gravelle did with AIDS research, and Sandy Jones with parenting, one of the advantages of being able to write well is having the option to open new doors when familiar ones are closed, or become so familiar the challenge is gone.

There is an endless variety of specialties in the freelance writing business. If the niche you are determined to target turns out to be a crowded field, there is no reason for despair. The trick, of course, is to do it better. That is the best kind of niche you can find.

WRITE A BUSINESS PLAN

Among the opportunities open to freelance writers is writing business plans for entrepreneurs starting new ventures. Even if you think of writing as a craft, a profession, or a calling, if you're planning to make a living at it, you need to regard yourself as an entrepreneur, too. And that means the most important business plan you can write is your own. Maybe for the first time in your life, you'll be writing about yourself. It's going to be a fascinating experience.

The easiest way to get started is to take a short vacation. Alone. Take along a bunch of yellow pads, a few pens, and an open mind. Then, as you relax by a pool, on a beach or next to a river or stream, take a hard look at where you want the future to take you. Go ahead and dream, but be completely honest with yourself. What you put on paper is going to help you follow your dream, and the last thing you need is to have your path skewed by things you really didn't believe in the first place.

START WITH THE OBVIOUS

Some of the questions you should ask yourself may seem pretty obvious, such as: "What sort of business am I planning?" and "What services am I going to offer?" But ask them anyway. No detail is too insignificant.

You should consider why there is a need for this business of yours, where you are going to find your clients, and how much you can expect them to pay for your services. Sure, you probably already have clients lined up, but you need to think about what you'll do if *their* business doesn't go according to plan.

You'll also need to make notes on the computer equipment and software you have, what you're going to need, and what it will probably cost. Unless you bought your computer last week, the one you have may already be obsolete. Nothing in this fast-changing world changes quite as often as computer hardware. You're going to be depending on that machine because if it breaks down, you're out of business.

Include in your business plan the investment you already made before you began dreaming this dream of yours. Even if you don't plan to buy a new computer, the one you have will be transformed from a toy into a business asset when you go out on your own.

Have you thought about offering desktop publishing services to some of your clients? If so, you may need graphics software and a course to bring you up to speed.

If you're planning to work at home, and nearly all freelance writers do, think about what it's going to cost you to create and furnish your home office. Even if you've already converted the front porch, write it down.

Your plan should include what other writers in your area have been up to, and what you're going to offer. You need to think about what kind of advertising and marketing it will take to find customers of your own. You may not consider other writers competition, but you should have a good idea who they are and what they do, especially the ones living in your immediate neighborhood. What you don't know can hurt you. If you are in a college town, for instance, there may be a graduate student willing to work at rates that would drive you to the poorhouse. Of course, you don't have any reason to believe that anything like that will happen to you, but common sense teaches us that what the competition is up to is an important part of a business plan.

THINK ABOUT THE MONEY

The most important thing you should consider is your financial plan, not just for this year, but for five years into the future. Many writers have low expectations about income. Money isn't as important as satisfaction, they believe, and they're convinced there is more of the latter than the former in the writing business. However, where is it written that a taxi driver is entitled to a higher income than a writer? Even if you don't think your expectations are too low, now is the time to raise them—before you start.

Your financial plan should begin with your start-up costs. Such items as the installation of a business telephone, insurance, accounting services, fees, and taxes all add up, and none of them should come as a surprise. Then project your operating costs, including supplies, utility bills, and personal and business taxes. And, whatever you do, don't forget to determine your living expenses.

Now think about the money you expect to make. Break down the business you anticipate on a weekly and monthly basis and translate those estimates into an income statement. From there, you'll be able to determine what it's going to take to reach a break-even point. It will also help you to predict profits and to avoid any cash-flow problems. Keep in mind that cash flow is what you're going to need to stay alive and ahead of the bill collectors. The profits are what will help make life worthwhile.

Freelance writers are fortunate because it doesn't take a lot of cash to be in business, but unless you've figured out how to get along without money, or don't mind spending the rest of your life worrying about it, you are going to need to assess your financial picture *before* you make a decision to go off on your own.

TESTING YOUR FINANCIAL READINESS

The following will help you gather the information you need *before* you get started. You may not have an immediate answer to every question in the questionnaire, written by career guidance professional Charles L. Sodikoff, Ph.D., and if you don't, ask your accountant or your friend at SCORE for help. Your financial analysis will be at the heart of your business plan.

DON'T LEAVE ANY STONES UNTURNED

Be specific and detailed with your answers, a plan based on dreams and not reality isn't worth the time it takes to write it down. Make sure your plan isn't so rigid that it can't be changed after you've started your business or that it is too vague to be helpful. It should tell you, and anyone else who reads it, where you want to go and, more important, how you expect to get there.

FINANCIAL READINESS

- What is the proper structure of your business? Should it be a sole proprietorship, a partnership, a limited liability company, or a corporation?
- How much money will it take to get your business started? What will you need to invest in equipment and supplies, setting up a work space, promotional materials, and fees?
- What type of insurance will you need? What will it cost?
- How much income do you need to support yourself (and your family) on a monthly basis?
- Where will you get the money? Have you explored all alternatives with a financial expert?
- How long do you anticipate it will take for your business to become profitable?
- How will you support yourself (and your family) until it starts making a profit? How long can you support yourself this way?
- How much can the business afford in overhead? What will your normal overhead be?
- Do you understand: Bookkeeping principles? Cash flow? Balance sheets? Profit-and-loss statements? Sales forecasting?
- How well do you know the market? Who will buy the things you write?
- Who is your competition? What will you do if more competitors arrive on the scene?
- What will you charge for your writing? What are your competitors charging?
- How will you deal with clients who don't pay you on time? Or not at all?

CHAPTER SIX

Getting Started

The basic tool of the writer's trade is what Hercule Poirot calls "little gray cells," and this isn't something you can go out and buy. You can enhance your brain power with education, and there are courses you can take to hone your skills or learn new ones, but writing may be the only profession there is with no basic boot camp such as law school or medical school. The *kind* of writing you do can be as varied as the shapes of snowflakes. So, apart from talent, training and experience, just what does it take to get started as a freelance writer? Not much in the way of tools and equipment, it turns out. As George Harrison of the Beatles was fond of pointing out, "It's all in the mind, you know."

That said, in this age of technology, there are some investments that you may need to make to get started, but these may not be as extensive as you think. Jim McClure, whose clients are mostly large Chicago-area telecommunications corporations, says, "I have better equipment right here in my house than most of the people I work with have in their offices." However, if you were to take a tour of Jim's home office you might wonder what he's talking about. His computer isn't brand-new, his modem isn't super-fast, his laser printer isn't state-of-the-art. He doesn't have a high-speed copying machine, he makes do with two telephone lines, and he doesn't have a fancy voice-mail system, just an old-fashioned answering machine. He does have a cellular phone, though, because, as he puts it, "I have to stay reachable. When a client calls, it's too easy for them to call someone else if I'm not at my desk."

Then what is it that makes him feel better-equipped than those high-powered executives who pride themselves on being technologically up-to-the-minute? "When you're dealing with corporate clients," he explains, "almost none of them has direct access to the Internet. Very few of them even have modems. They are hooked up through corporate LANs—local area networks—and all they have is access to internal E-mail. It's just about impossible for an outside freelancer to get through the firewalls of those corporate systems. And none of them would work with anybody who couldn't hand-deliver jobs on computer disks."

Like everything else, the world of freelance writing has changed since the days writers pounded away on their typewriters. Some writers even wrote everything on yellow pads and had secretaries transcribe their output, but these days, if you could find a typewriter in the first place, you probably couldn't find ribbons for it. And where in the world would you find a secretary? Even if you could afford one.

Almost nobody, from book publishers to advertising agencies, will accept copy or manuscripts thick with White-Out these days. And if you remember a time when writers used a pair of scissors and a roll of Scotch tape to reorganize their work, that's out, too. Whatever you write, it needs to be submitted as pristine hard copy and a computer file, either on a disk or as an E-mail transmission. Editors don't use blue pencils any longer.

However, when you set yourself up for business, it's still a simple case of less is more. Just be sure you can deliver your work in a form clients in every field are demanding these days. As Jim McClure noted, that means computer disks, and unless you're working with Internet-deprived corporate types, you're also going to want to have a way to send computer files electronically.

Obviously, that means you need a computer. You probably already have one, but since you're planning to restart your life with a clean slate, you might want to find out what's different out there since the last time you looked. Your computer is going to become as important to your new life as a car in suburbia, and you're going to need it to be trouble-free.

TAKE A SHOPPING TRIP

Even if you don't think you're going to need to buy one, computer shopping is something like going to a boat show—and every bit as much fun. Nearly everything you see will tempt you, but it's simple to talk yourself out of buying everything you see. When all is said and done, you don't really need much equipment to handle a freelance writing business. On the other hand, that may be a good reason to go for the best you can afford.

One thing that may surprise you if you haven't explored this world in a while is the prices. Yes, computers still aren't cheap, but prices are dropping and the list of features is going up, almost on a daily basis.

When you go computer shopping, you'll find that prices vary from catalog to catalog and from store to store (you may even find that the price on the shelf is negotiable!). It's a good idea to shop around, but bargains aren't the only thing you should be looking for. A computer that's short on memory or isn't compatible with the software you need now or in the future isn't worth the space it takes up on your desk.

You are going to meet some computer salespeople who will remind you of used car salesmen, which may be why the industry term for them is "resellers." Of course, you can expect them to know a lot about their products, and you can learn a lot by listening to them, but don't let them talk you into buying equipment you don't need or can't use. Do your homework first. Talk with people who use computers as well as the ones who sell them. Take a trip on the Internet and visit computer-related websites. Read computer magazines and newspapers and send away for information from their advertisers. At the very least, after you've absorbed enough of that information, you might find yourself qualified to be a technical writer. And, as you'll see, the computer world constitutes an immense market for them.

YOU CAN TAKE IT WITH YOU

Among the advantages of being a freelance writer is that you can work just about anywhere at all, especially if you have a laptop computer. In advertising its offerings in the portable field, IBM may have had you in mind with its invitation to "use it where you think best." These machines, which were once to desktop computers what portable typewriters were to IBM Selectrics, have been dramatically improved over recent years, and there isn't much you can't accomplish with one. Most laptops weigh seven or eight pounds, many newer models are even lighter, but sometimes you may want add-on drives, which will add to their heft, as will AC power supplies. The current generation of laptops generally has all the power and features you need already built in, but if you find you are going to want to add to it, be careful to buy products that are compatible. You can do very well with a fifteen-hundred-dollar investment in a machine that comes with a four-gigabyte hard drive, a CD-ROM player, and a modem, although prices for a speedier laptop can run up to six thousand. However, as with everything else in the computer business, the prices are dropping.

For speed, common wisdom has it that your laptop needs to have an Intel-based system. In fact, a rumor around Silicon Valley a few years ago was that when Apple founder Steve Jobs bought a laptop for his college-bound daughter, it was an IBM ThinkPad. But whether that's true or not, Macintosh has been steadily catching up since then and its newer PowerBooks are actually faster than the competition. Then again, there are other features to consider besides speed, so even if you believe a laptop computer will make your life easier, don't buy the first one you see.

If you haven't checked out laptops lately, among the improvements you'll see are batteries that last longer than they used to. But no matter how sophisticated the technology has become, they are still batteries and are prone to running out of juice at the worst possible time. When that happens, the computer slows down and then stops, no matter what kind of chip is inside. An event like that can take all the joy out of being able to work on your manuscript under a beach umbrella. A way to limit the problem, if not avoid it altogether, is to buy lithium replacement batteries. They cost more, something like two hundred twenty-five dollars compared to one hundred seventy-five for NiMH (nickel and metal hydride) technology, but they last longer. Many of the new laptops come with lithium batteries as original equipment.

The laptop's battery gauge is designed to tell you how much power you have available, but it may not be as reliable as you've been led to believe. When in doubt, plug it in. And when you leave home, take along a spare battery and consider investing in an external battery recharger. And, remember, the battery drains even when you have the laptop's power turned off, so when you're not using it, keep it plugged in! About once a month or so, you should "burp" your battery—that is, let it run dry and then recharge it fully. Leave the AC adapter turned on and take the battery out for about thirty seconds. Then replace it and recharge it. The average laptop battery is good for about five hundred rechargings.

Although laptop computers are not as sturdy as other computers, they are, of course, very similar. There are, however, some differences you should consider. Lower-cost models are equipped with "passive-matrix" screens, sometimes called "dual-scan," which require adjusting the first time you turn them on. In some cases, illumination on these screens is uneven and sometimes there are annoying shadow images to contend with. You may even find at times it is difficult to keep track of the cursor.

Passive-matrix laptops also have a narrow viewing angle, which means that if you're not looking straight at the screen, you'll see a murky image at best, or possibly nothing at all. If you're spending alot of time working on your laptop, take frequent breaks. The limited viewing angle can force you to sit in one position for too long, and you may begin to feel a nagging pain between your shoulders. The narrow viewing angle can also be a problem if a client is looking over your shoulder to see what you're doing.

You don't have to be worried about the health effects of spending a lot of time too close to a laptop computer screen. These thin, flat screens use a technology called LCD (liquid crystal display) like your digital watch. There are no electrical emissions from them, so there is no radiation danger. Illumination is lower than with desktop screens, so if you spend long hours staring at the screen, eyestrain could be a problem. Some desktops are already available with LCD screens, which save huge amounts of desk space. Needless to say, they are quite expensive. But count on it, prices will drop and one of these days it's a sure bet that LCD will be the standard for all computer screens.

"Active-matrix" screens, are generally more expensive because they are produced abroad and subject to higher import duties than most other electronic equipment. However, they come equipped with brightness and contrast controls and the picture is much sharper. Better still, you can see it from the side, which is good news for your aching back, though you may not find the added cost worthwhile.

If you're considering using a laptop computer for all your work, keep in mind that the screen is smaller, which means you're going to have to do more scrolling to keep track of the things you are writing. The keyboard is smaller as well, and harder for some people to manipulate than a desktop system.

No matter how convenient a portable computer may be, many people who use them also have desktop models and transfer files from laptop to desktop. There are several ways this is accomplished, including moving files back and forth on a floppy disk, but among the easiest of them for average users is to have a permanent docking station. If you are going on a trip, you don't need to carry extra drives you won't need, and when you get back to the office you simply attach the laptop to its dock where such things as a big color monitor and full keyboard allow you to use your laptop as a regular desktop without investing in two machines. However, the newer generations of laptops are as fully equipped as many desktops in terms of memory and other features, so unless you're interested in keyboard comfort and the convenience of a bigger color monitor, you probably won't want to spend the extra money on a docking station.

WHAT SHOULD IT BE: MAC OR PC?

Researching computer-related information is probably the simplest kind of digging you can do. The world of computers is filled with experts who seem to find sharing information a joyful experience, but there is one question that will never get you a simple answer: Should you to buy Apple Macintosh or IBM-compatible hardware?

The people who prefer one over the other are like religious fanatics, and they'll do everything they can to convert you to their way of thinking. When all is said and done however, the choice you'll make is a very personal one, and may depend on your past experience with computers. Nevertheless, it is imperative that your system, and its software, is compatible with the platforms your clients are using.

There was once a time when an IBM machine would clam up like a kid faced with a plate of spinach when it was fed an Apple disk, and the reverse was also true. Newer computers have eliminated the problem, but it still takes a bit of coaxing before one will recognize the competition, and it's best to be able to give your clients files they can use without too much bother.

In general, most corporations and other large businesses are IBM-equipped; book publishers, ad agencies, and other clients that use extensive graphics are more likely to be using Macs. Of course, since the introduction of Microsoft Windows, the graphics capabilities of the IBM PC and its clones have become more like Macs, if not still harder to learn. Any IBM fan will be quick to tell you that there is more software available for their preferred platform, but Mac people will respond that they're referring to video games and that such things have nothing to do with your business. On the other hand, if you're using the latest versions of Microsoft Word, the most popular word processing program, you'll probably find that it is more IBM-friendly.

YOUR CONSTANT COMPANION

Like most other fields, the computer business has a language all its own and, like traveling in a foreign country, it's a good idea to learn a few of the key words before beginning your tour of the land of the resellers. It may be helpful even if you don't plan to invest in anything new. Certainly, you're not expected to be able to take your machine apart and put it back together again like a Marine with his rifle, but you're going to be sharing your life with a computer from now on, and it doesn't hurt to be able to understand the language.

The most basic of the terms in computerspeak is CPU. It is the central processing unit that makes software able to do its job.

Its main storage area is a fixed internal magnetic disk known as a hard drive, whose capacity grows with every new model. A hard drive memory measured in megabytes was standard up through the early nineties, and one hundred twenty of them seemed to be about as much as anyone would ever need, but it isn't at all uncommon for newer models to boast four gigabytes of hard drive memory, and some start out with as many as nine.

And what, you might ask, is the difference between a megabyte and a gigabyte? It all begins as a byte, a combination of adjacent bits of computer language that form a character—that is, one letter, number, or punctuation mark. A bit, which purists call a binary digit, is the single basic unit of information fed into a computer.

Floppy disks and other storage devices with a capacity of less than a million characters are measured in kilobytes, a thousand bytes at a time, designated by an upper-case K (800K = 800,000 bytes). Above a million bytes, the designation becomes M or MB for megabytes, and a thousand MB becomes GB, or, more formally, a gigabyte. Sometime in the not too distant future, you'll probably be hearing about terabytes, which is another thousand megabytes bigger than a gigabyte, but don't worry about that now, unless you're planning to store the Library of Congress on your hard drive.

One of the ways megabytes haunt people who do design work on their computers is when they relate to RAM, random access memory. Graphics programs such as Photoshop eat up those megs like salted nuts. You may be thinking that you're lucky not to have to worry about that, but even word processing programs rely on having plenty of RAM available. Your computer uses it to keep track of information while you're working on it. The CPU takes care of problem-solving, but it sends the data you're feeding it to the RAM, where it is stored as "cache memory," which keeps track of it as you go along. The more the cache can store, the faster the computer will do what you need it to do.

Although it's axiomatic for computer buyers that you can never have too much RAM, for word processing you probably won't need more than thirty-two megabytes or for a little more horsepower on the Internet, sixty-four megabytes should do the trick.

And while you're planning ahead, you may want to consider expanding your service, and adding to your income, by providing things like newsletters or other graphic elements to your capabilities. If that interests you, you'll need to add a graphics program, and the highest amount of RAM you can afford. If you are on a tight budget, check to see if you can add more RAM later. Even if you don't think you'll ever use your computer for anything but word processing, lots of RAM means you'll be able to work faster—and easier, too.

WHAT MORE DO YOU NEED?

Computer salesmen may try to talk you into big storage systems such as zip, or cartridge drives such as jaz, but unless you're writing an encyclopedia, or plan on doing graphics work, you don't need them. You may find such a system useful for storing or backing up your files, but if you are just producing average-size documents, a box of high-density floppy disks will serve you very well for a small fraction of the price.

Do remember to save your text constantly and back up your work at the end of each day. When your computer loses electrical power, it forgets what it was doing and chances are when you get it running again you'll have to rely on your own memory to pick up the thread. How much time can you afford to spend recovering lost ideas? It's a choice between one preventive keystroke and a mountain of aggravation.

At the end of the day, you should put each *job* on a separate disk as well. Consider it your file copy. When the work is paid for and printed, and you have a floppy disk safely in your file cabinet, you can remove the job file from your hard disk and free up some space.

Whatever your storage system or how often you save your files, never plug your computer into anything but a surge protector. If an unexpected storm jolts your system, not only do you risk a morning's work but anything else on your hard drive as well. Much better than an ordinary surge protector is an uninterrupted power supply (UPS). For as little as a hundred dollars a UPS provides protection for your whole system from the computer itself to your modem, your printer, your fax machine and storage drives. Not only that, but it suppresses surges in telephone lines when you're online. Many models will also automatically save data and shut down the computer when the power fails.

Naturally, you need a monitor, but you don't need anything fancy for word processing. You don't even need it to display color images, but you'd probably have to scour junkyards to find a black-and-white one. Something you should consider, though, is that a larger screen may be worthwhile in cutting down your scrolling time. The fifteen-inch monitors that come with most computer packages don't display a full page of text at one time, and you'll find yourself scrolling back and forth to see what you've been saying. Beyond that, when you shop for a monitor, the best thing to do is simply look at the screen to see for yourself what you'll be looking at every day for a long time to come. Eyestrain shouldn't be an occupational disease you'll have to deal with.

Nor should carpal tunnel syndrome, a painful wrist-nerve disorder that strikes computer users. The keyboard you select—and there are dozens to choose from—will help you avoid it, so road-test a few for comfort before you buy one. It's also well worth investing in a hand rest, or a keyboard that has one built into it. A twist of the wrist can put you out of business.

Computer makers consider printers an optional extra, even though you can't function without one. They can reproduce in black-and-white or color and they come in three types: dot-matrix, inkjet, and laser. The print quality of dot-matrix printers tends to be ragged, and not recommended as a way to put your best face forward. Besides, the cost of better-quality inkjet printers keeps dropping, and their noisy, slow, dot-matrix cousins are quickly becoming museum pieces. A dot-matrix printer is a lot like an old-fashioned typewriter, right down to the ribbon. You still see them in computer stores and catalogs because they are excellent for printing multiple-copy forms as well as checks, receipts, and other business documents.

A laser printer works like a Xerox machine, using a laser diode to transfer an image to a cylindrical drum that uses an electrostatic process to attract toner particles (the powder that creates the printout) and fuses them to the page with heated rollers. Some are better than others, but it takes a laser printer to deliver the best possible quality. But that doesn't mean you need one, unless your computer printouts are going to be used as art for a commercial printer.

If you work with photographs, a new breed of flatbed scanner not only gets the images into your computer but doubles as a laser printer, copier, and a fax machine as well. When you're shopping for one, remember that a copier and a printer aren't the same thing. All scanners function as copiers, but only the more expensive ones also incorporate a printer. You can also use them to scan text into your computer. A budget version of this multitalented machine is priced well below three hundred dollars, but even the best of them come in at around a thousand.

When all is said and done, though, you'll get along very well with an inkjet printer to create the clean hard copy you need, and you probably don't have to go to the expense of buying one that prints in color. There are many variations on the inkjet theme as newer technology brings them closer to laser-quality. Among the leaders in this quest for more color and realism is the Canon Corporation, whose Bubblejet printers print color photographs almost as close to the original as the output of more expensive laser printers.

If you get an inkjet printer, make sure you have a spare ink supply in your desk. These printers spray ink onto the page from a sealed cartridge, but very few will warn you when they're running dry. They just spew out blank pages as if nothing has happened.

Just as important as print quality is printing speed. Keep it in mind when you're looking at printers because, while most computers have a "background printing" feature that allows you to get on with your work while a document is being printed, there will be times when you want that printed copy right now and you'll be grateful for a speedy response.

Most computers come equipped with CD-ROM drives these days (shorthand for "compact disk read-only memory"). You need one, because a lot of software and reference material is now delivered only on CD-ROMS.

A scanner allows you to import images into your computer so they can be integrated into the text. You may not need one for the kind of work you'll be doing, but if you would like to import large amounts of text rather than typing it in, a scanner with an OCR program (optical character recognition) will save you a lot of time and effort. The OCR program allows the scanner to differentiate between words and pictures and lets you scan printed pages which you can import into your word processing program. When you shop for one, though, be careful to look for the best quality. It is also important to go for the highest dpi (dots per inch) rating you can afford. If your scanner can't tell the difference between an "n" or an "r" it's going to be more trouble than it's worth. When you go to the computer store, take along a floppy disk and a newspaper classified page (the one with jobs for writers). Run the page through the scanner, copy it to the disk, and take it home to see how it looks on your own screen.

GET CONNECTED

The most basic and essential of the freelance writer's tools has become Internet access and E-mail capability. And for that you're going to need a modem (an abbreviation of the technical term modulator-demodulator) to get connected. Most modems transmit through telephone lines at 9,600 or 14,400 bits per second, which is known as the baud rate. You'll see numbers as high as 57,600 bps, which means that the modem is capable of compressing the data it sends so it will take less time. A higher baud rate will allow you to cruise the Internet at higher speeds, although there are variables, such as the efficiency of the online service you are using and the limitations of your telephone line. However, for faxing, your modem can only be as fast as the one at the other end of the line.

You should also have a separate phone line for your modem. When your phone is connected to your computer, you can't receive calls.

Many modems also double as a fax machine, another tool you should have, but most won't receive a fax if the computer isn't turned on, so if you expect to get faxes in the middle of the night or on your day off, it's a good idea to also put a standard fax machine on your shopping list. Invest in a plain-paper fax so you can use it like a copying machine to reproduce letters and other documents.

A copying machine may be an expense you can avoid. There are more places to have copies made in most neighborhoods than there are barbershops. And if you're copying long documents, it's cheaper to let the copyshop handle them than to eat into your own time.

YOUR WORKPLACE

Debra Jason shares an office in Boulder with several other creative people, and says, "We're like a virtual agency. I share jobs with my designer neighbors, and we all recommend each other for jobs." Other freelance writers have an outside office because they want to be accessible to their clients, share a receptionist, or have a professional address.

But these are the rare exceptions in the world of freelance writing. Running their businesses from their homes is one thing nearly all independent writers have in common, and it makes good sense. A freelance writing business doesn't take up a lot of space, and working at home cuts the cost of overhead. Even though not everyone finds that living and working in the same place is the best way to run a business, most writers seem to find it an amicable match. For one thing, it can give them uninterrupted time to get their work done, and you certainly can't beat the rent.

However, when you put together your home office, be careful not to confuse your two lives. Your work space may be under the same roof as your bed and your breakfast nook, but you need to think of it as a completely different world. That's what the IRS expects you to do, and even if you've got files and books and papers strewn all over the house, this isn't going to cut it with them. It shouldn't with you, either. You will be working to make a living, but don't make the mistake of living with your work.

To paraphrase the sign over the salad bar, take all the space you need, but use the space you take—and not a square foot more. Don't let your work spill over into your living space. And those magazines and computer printouts belong near your desk and not on the coffee table in the living room. Be obsessive about it. Your business will infiltrate your personal life if you're not.

And you know what they say about all work and no play—it makes for a dull life.

It is important to have a separate telephone line for your business, too (no, not the one connected to your modem, a *different* one). That way, you'll always be sure it will be answered in a professional way and, besides, it's easier. The IRS requires you to keep business and personal calls separate in your tax records.

Keep your business phone lines in the part of the house where you'll be doing business because that is where your records and logs ought to be. Apart from having one of the kids answering your business telephone, one of the most unprofessional things you can do is to ask a client to hold the phone while you run from the kitchen to your office to look something up.

It goes without saying that when a client calls, you should be able to put your finger on the correct file without a long search. That means you have to keep your workspace organized. You might think that since your office is your private domain, neatness doesn't count. You may even have a sign there that says "A sloppy desk is a sign of a creative mind," but don't believe a word of it. Let your creativity show in your work, not on your desk.

That isn't to say that your office should look like you're expecting a photographer from a decorating magazine to drop by. However, suppose a client calls out of the blue to talk about a contract. Your mind is lost in the job on which you're working and you can't for the life of you put your hands on that piece of paper, but for the life of your business, you'd better be able to. If your office isn't organized, you won't be either. And if you're not organized, you're not only going to waste time but miss opportunities, too.

Bill Allen, who writes articles for in-flight magazines, lives pretty close to the New York Public Library. "I used to enjoy going there," he says, "but I haven't had the pleasure in a long, long time." Jim uses the World Wide Web to satisfy all his research needs. In fact, of the forty-plus writers interviewed for this book, only Lisa Kirazian, a Los Angeles–based grant writer, said that she uses her local library for more than occasional fact-checking. "In my business, I need to keep up with trends in the arts," she says, "and I go the library to read magazines." But if push came to shove, Lisa could probably find most of those magazines online. Bill Allen routinely uses Compuserve's magazine database, and sometimes even runs across his own work there.

Research is only one reason why you should have online access, however. Being able to E-mail files to your clients saves an incredible amount of time. An entire book manuscript can be sent to an editor in less time than it takes to fill out the form to send it overnight.

And there's another reason, too. One of the most difficult transitions people experience when they shift from working in an office to working alone at home is not having interaction with other people for help and encouragement. It is especially true of writing, which can be a lonely experience even for newspaper reporters working in noisy newsrooms. Many freelance writers have found a way around it by chatting online with other writers.

For doing research on the Web, you probably need a good Internet server that will help you skirt around the ads and the noise of a service like America Online, MSN, or Compuserve. But these servers give you Web access, too, and their chat rooms and newsgroups will help you get in on the fun of keeping in touch.

SOFTWARE

It's against the rules to rent, borrow, or steal software, but even if it weren't forbidden to copy someone else's programs, it isn't a very good idea. The technical support that software developers provide to registered owners through their 800 numbers and the manuals you get when you buy their programs are worth their weight in gold. When you're on a deadline and a software glitch pops up unexpectedly, you're going to be grateful for the help, but don't forget to fill out the registration forms that come with them, and keep the registration numbers handy—they're your passwords to the help lines.

For a freelance writer, a word processing program just about says it all. There are several to chose from, but far and away the most popular is Microsoft Word. The instruction manual that comes with it is close to nine hundred pages long, and you can take courses to delve into all its intricacies. But by and large, once it's installed on your hard drive, using it is as simple as typing. There are even simpler programs that can do the job, of course. But since word processing is basic to your business, you'll get better results from Word or another super word-cruncher such as WordPerfect. And, more likely than not, you'll be compatible with your clients.

Once you get comfortable with one of those programs, you'll find there isn't much you won't be able to do. However, if you want to do more, creating a storyboard for a TV commercial you've written, for instance, you might want to add a graphics program to your bag of tricks. To offer desktop publishing services, page layout programs such as QuarkXpress and PageMaker will probably be the most useful in the beginning. They allow you to create the basic format of a document, a magazine page, or a newsletter, say, and to import text and other graphic elements into it as they are created.

Other graphics facilitators, which may not be as useful to a writer, are illustration programs such as FreeHand and Illustrator which produce original artwork; and image editing programs such as Photoshop and ClarisWorks, which allow for the retouching and altering of photographs a dot (pixel) at a time. But unless you have a lot of time, a lot of patience and a lot of RAM, you're probably better off leaving those to the art department.

CAN YOU GO IT ALONE?

A freelance writer is like a one-man band, doing everything from drumming up business to taking the applause for a job well done. And by definition, that's the way it will always be. If you start hiring other writers to expand your business, you'll end up with an ad agency or a literary agency instead of a freelance writing business.

There will be times when you'll be overloaded and have to shift assignments to another writer, but then it usually becomes their job and not yours. The business you're considering has just one product to sell: *your* talent and *your* personal approach to solving a client's problems.

Does that mean you're not going to need any outside help? Not exactly.

WILL YOU NEED A LAWYER?

How many writers do you know who have lawyers? Very few seem to. It's probably because of what the psychological testers call their subjective personalities. Hard-shell individualists, as most writers seem to be, don't usually welcome advice about their work, and certainly not about how to live their lives. However, it might be a good idea to come out of your shell for a little advice because you need to protect yourself and your personal assets. As one lawyer explains it, "if your business fails, you can lose your house, your car and everything you own unless you take the right steps before you start. And that includes setting up some form of corporation to protect yourself."

You probably won't need to keep an attorney at your beck and call, but it is a good idea to consult one at first to make sure you don't get off on the wrong foot. There are important things to consider, such as which form of business is best for you. There will be legal papers to file at the start, too. And, most important of all, every writing job you take on should begin with a written contract, and you will need professional advice in drafting a form that makes sure all the bases are covered, including ways to avoid collection problems. Obviously, you won't need to consult with a lawyer on every job, but it's a good idea to have one help you develop some guidelines in the beginning.

Among the best reasons for having a lawyer handy is copyright law. No matter how you slice it, a great deal of what freelance writers do is *rewriting*. Generally speaking, you are free to quote small portions of most previously published material as long as you credit the source. Historical facts are usually fair game, too, as long you know they're facts and present them in your own way. You can even use long passages from writing that is in public domain. But how do you know what is? The laws are changing, but for now a copyright lasts an author's lifetime plus fifty years, and in most cases anything written before the 1920s is probably in the public domain and copyright-free. But what if you, knowingly or unknowingly, extract someone else's ideas? You might find yourself hearing from someone else's lawyer.

Consider quoting song lyrics, for instance. It can get you into a lot of trouble unless you go way back to songs like "Sweet Adeline" or "If You Don't Like My Peaches, Why Do You Shake My Tree?" However, if you love a Gershwin tune, the going rate to use one in a television advertising campaign can be as high as a quarter million dollars. It would cost a whole lot less to use Ira Gershwin's words in a book or an article, of course, but don't try it without getting legal advice first.

Libel laws might haunt you in a costly way. Sometimes something that seems innocuous to you, could offend someone and have them reaching for the phone to call their lawyer. Your best insurance against such a thing is to check with your own lawyer before the piece is published. At all costs you want to avoid the possibility of lawsuits, so look for a lawyer who not only understands your business, but has experience with copyright and libel laws.

The best place to find a lawyer with this specialty is by calling the local Bar Association. In most places, they'll provide you with a list of attorneys in your area whose experience best suits your needs, and they'll give you some idea of how much you can expect to pay. You can also ask other writers or people with small businesses for recommendations, or your accountant, who may know of a lawyer who is familiar with the business of writing. The experts at SCORE will be helpful, too, particularly if your budget is limited.

Legal fees vary from area to area and from lawyer to lawyer, and, everything else being equal, it pays to do a little comparison shopping. You may find that you'll only need to pay a small fee for the paperwork you need to get started, but you will pay by the hour for a consultation. With that in mind, you ought to have some idea what your options are before you sit down in a lawyer's office. To make sure you'll be able to touch all the bases in short order, go there with a written list of questions.

WHAT FORM SHOULD YOUR BUSINESS TAKE?

Most freelance writers operate as though they were still on someone else's payroll. Their businesses are usually called "sole proprietorships," although accountants often refer to them as "Schedule C" businesses for the federal income tax forms they need to fill out, but the problem with a proprietorship is that your personal assets and your business assets get all mixed up. In addition, your spouse's assets are mixed in there, too, which may be taking more of a chance on love than either of you bargained for.

As far as the tax people are concerned, as a sole proprietor, your income from your business is no different than if you were earning a salary. It's the same with your creditors. Your business debts are the same to them as your personal ones, and if your business gets into trouble (yes, it can happen even to freelance writers), you might find your personal bank accounts frozen. You need to have a way to separate business from pleasure or you can lose everything you own whether it has anything to do with your business or not.

A legal partnership, like a sole proprietorship, makes no distinction between your personal and business assets, nor is your liability limited to your original investment. And to make matters worse, you don't have the same amount of control over your finances because you have a partner's input to contend with. If your company runs into financial trouble and your partners can't help you pay the bills, you will be left holding the bag.

Chances are you aren't thinking of forming a partnership anyway, and even though you may be thinking big, forming a corporation is probably out of the question, too. In the world of big business, investors form corporations and declare themselves shareholders as a kind of ultimate protection from personal risk. If the corporation goes bankrupt, they are not responsible for anything beyond their original investment, but before you consider issuing stock in your new venture, you need to consider the downside. It's a big one. You'll owe the federal government a huge tax on any profits you make, and many states will levy their own corporate tax on top of that. If you pay yourself any dividends, you'll have to report them on your personal income tax return, and that means you will be paying taxes on money that has already been taxed.

Still, when you become a freelance writer, you are forming a business whether you think of it that way or not and you need the protection that comes with formalizing it. And this may be simpler than you imagined.

For small businesses like yours, the IRS has come up with a different kind of structure it calls Subchapter S. It gives you all the benefits of being incorporated, without most of the burdens. Basically, Subchapter S allows business and professional people to be considered a corporation, except when the time comes to pay the taxes. Subchapter S companies don't pay corporate income taxes on their profits. Instead, their owners are taxed just once, on April 15. They are allowed to deduct business losses and expenses, which can reduce personal income taxes, especially at the beginning when they are reinvesting their profits in the business. There are some restrictions in the Subchapter S scenario, but not many of them will have any effect on your freelance writing business.

There are even fewer limitations with a new kind of business form that has come on the scene, a limited liability company, which offers the same protection that investors in large corporations enjoy, but is taxed like a partnership or a sole proprietorship. Like a partnership, they have a predetermined life, usually thirty years, which can be extended. And in some states, though not all, they need to have the earmarks of a partnership with a requirement that at least two persons form the company.

A limited liability company might be the best way for you to go. The revised federal tax law of 1996 made Subchapter S companies more like LLCs, but there still are differences; those that will affect you when you're starting up your new business are more likely to be on the local level. Some states don't recognize the Subchapter S concept, for instance, and they tax such companies as unincorporated businesses.

Because there are so many variables, you *absolutely* must talk to your lawyer or your accountant about them before you make a decision—not only can it save you money every tax year, but it will protect your personal assets as well.

SHOULD YOU JOIN A UNION?

On the other hand, once you've consulted a lawyer to help you get your ducks in a row, you may be able to get most of the legal help you need by joining a union. There are dozens of unions and professional organizations out there, and the choice you make depends on what kind of writing you do.

Among the biggest is the Authors Guild (E-mail: staff@ authorsguild.org), which has been representing writers for more than eighty years. Its legal staff reviews publishing and agent's contracts on an individual basis for its seven thousand writer-members, and follows-up for them when things go wrong. The guild also publishes a quarterly newsletter, and provides online services as well as access to a wide range of insurance plans from life policies to dental coverage.

Membership, which costs ninety dollars for the first year, is open to any author who has had a book published by an American publisher in the last seven years or three works of fiction or nonfiction published in a general circulation periodical in the last year and a half. Authors with contracts for as-yet-unpublished work qualify for associate membership.

Membership in the American Society of Journalists and Authors (E-mail: asja@compuserve.com) is open to independent freelance nonfiction writers. You qualify if you've written six articles for national periodicals, regional magazines, or newspapers, or two nonfiction books. There is a twenty-five-dollar application fee, which is applied to the initiation fee of one hundred dollars when your application is accepted. Annual dues are one hundred sixty-five dollars.

Among the benefits of ASJA membership is inclusion in the database for its "Dial-a-Writer" service, which helps potential clients locate you. Another opportunity for members is ASJA's "WriteSpeakers" referral service, which can put you in touch with event-planners looking for speakers on topics you may have mastered. In some cases, the fees can be as high fifteen thousand dollars—not a bad day's work for something you've been talking about every day anyway.

The National Writers Union (E-mail: NWU@netcom.com) is more like a trade union than most other organizations established for writers. It offers grievance resolution to specific problems and help in negotiating contracts. Its membership, which ranges from academic authors and poets to cartoonists and copywriters, is open to anyone who has published a book, a play, three articles, five poems, or the equivalent in other kinds of writing. Even unpublished writers are welcome, based on the same general formula, as long as they are attempting to sell their work.

In addition to group health insurance, the NWU also maintains a database of literary agents for its members, and job hotlines, both nationwide for technical writing and regionally, for freelance writing opportunities. Its Internet chat sites and E-mail lists also give you ample opportunities for networking. Membership dues range from ninety dollars a year if your writing income is under five thousand dollars, to one hundred ninety-five dollars if you earn more than twenty-five thousand dollars a year as a writer.

If you are writing screenplays or television scripts, you'll benefit from membership in the Writers Guild of America, which negotiates agreements with producers as well as individual contracts for members involved in television news. Eligibility is based on having sold literary material to a company that has signed its agreement and there is a fifteen-hundred-dollar initiation fee for freelancers.

But if that gleam in your eye is the germ of a screenplay or a novel, you should know about WGA's script registration service, which is available to nonmembers. (Get an overview on the Internet at http://www.wgaeast.org/) Basically, it involves sealing your manuscript (or a synopsis, a treatment, an outline or an idea) in an envelope, filling out a form and mailing or delivering it to a WGA office. For a small fee, the sealed envelope will be registered and kept on file for ten years. It is intended to give you proof of authorship, if not legal protection and, in the film business at least, agents and producers will not even look at scripts that haven't first been registered with the Writers Guild.

WILL YOU NEED AN ACCOUNTANT?

Very few writers say they use an accountant for anything more than handling their tax returns. Some find it helpful to check in with one every couple of months to make sure that their actual income is squaring with the estimate they made last April. If it isn't, an accountant can decide if it is worthwhile to adjust their quarterly estimated payments to the IRS and avoid an unexpected bill next April. The same road check, by the way, can also reduce your quarterly payments if you're not making money as fast as you thought you would.

Some freelance writers use financial software on their computers to do the work of an accountant, but most say they prefer going to a professional. Susan Abbott, who writes newsletters in her Twin Cities home office, is among them. She hired an accountant to help her set up her books and to show her how use them. He reviews her books every quarter and also helps her with her taxes. She says she couldn't get along without the service, particularly because "the local sales tax is a gray area here in St. Paul. I have to collect it and pay it." It's one more time-consuming detail she'd rather not have to deal with.

Irwin Fenishel, a New York City accountant, says that most small business people like freelance writers use his services for taxes, financial statements, and bookkeeping. In his experience, most entrepreneurial types "have a careless attitude about money." (Sound like anybody *you* know?) He says that he finds that most of them have more faith in the future than they probably should, and don't usually care about going into debt to get them past the rough spots because they believe they're going to hit it big one of these days. It may be a great outlook on life, but, as he puts it, "they need an accountant to rein them in a little."

When he works with a new small business start-up, his key consideration is capital and financing. In just about every kind of small business, including freelance writing where not much investment is required, there can be long months at the beginning when there is no money coming in to take care of daily expenses. He wants to be sure a new businessperson will be able to deal with it, because there is often nowhere for them to turn for help. "Banks aren't very comfortable with new businesses," he warns, "and even less so with service businesses like writing."

When he studies a client's financial statements, the most important thing he looks for is debt to equity because "a heavily leveraged business has a serious problem." He also looks carefully at business plans with special attention to projections. "Banks do, too," he adds.

He also warns that banks generally require a personal guarantee for loans, especially for first-time borrowers. This means that if you're thinking of applying for a loan with a bank, you may be required to provide collateral, such as your home or personal and business assets, to guarantee the loan. Because the value of computer equipment drops so rapidly, it is generally not accepted as collateral.

As for hiring an accountant, he advises that "it's a two-way street. Both parties need to comfortable with one another, and I need to feel I can recommend a client to a bank when they need help."

MONEY MATTERS

Without an accountant, you may have a hard time keeping up with all the information crucial to the life of your business—such as expenses and accounts receivable. Your accountant can help you determine how much cash flow you need to stay afloat, and blow the whistle when money isn't coming in fast enough. If you find you need a loan to keep you going, your accountant will put together the paperwork the lender wants to see, plus give you advice about what sort of loan to ask for, what protection you need, and where to take your application.

ARE YOU INSURED FOR THAT?

Either your lawyer or your accountant can be helpful in recommending the kinds of insurance you should have. Some liability insurance plans are available with riders that can protect you against judgments in lawsuits, for instance. You'll need protection against fire and theft, too, but, most important of all, you'll certainly need a medical insurance policy, preferably one that will help keep your business functioning—and your family fed—if you need hospitalization. In addition to losing a steady paycheck when you strike out on your own, you're also losing all those benefits that come with a steady job. There is no such thing as a sick day when you're in business for yourself.

Many freelance writers have medical insurance through working spouses, but they're the lucky ones. What if you're single or supporting a family on your own? Health insurance rates for individuals can sometimes be as high as the mortgage on your house. And, like the house, you can't get along without it.

Being part of a group is one way to cut the expense. Organizations like the National Writers Union and the Authors Guild offer access to lower-cost coverage. You might also try networking among small business owners in your neighborhood as well.

In some areas, established business organizations or the local chamber of commerce offer health coverage at group rates.

You can also cut the cost of medical insurance by going for a high-deductible policy. The premiums are lower, but remember that you will be paying more money to a doctor or hospital when you use it.

When you announce that you are open for business, you can count on getting letters and phone calls from all kinds of people trying to sell you something, and medical insurance is high on the list, but be careful not to buy anything from anyone unless you have every reason to believe you are dealing with a reputable company, no matter how attractive the rate might seem. Remember the old rule that if it seems to be too good to be true, it probably is.

You may also want to consider investing in a pension plan so you can retire someday, and if you expect to have clients visiting your office, liability insurance might be a good idea. Whatever your insurance needs, the good news is that it is all available from a single source, a good insurance agent. Like travel agents, these people don't charge fees either for advice or for looking out for your changing needs. Their income is from commissions on the premiums you pay, year in and year out, so your insurance agent can be expected to be at your service as long as you're in business.

Be careful how you choose one. Look for an insurance agent who represents more than one company. Many do, and that gives you the advantage of comparing costs and coverages without going to several different sources. You'll also want an agent who is familiar with small businesses (particularly the business of writing) and can anticipate your needs. Chances are the person who sold you life insurance and your homeowner's policy won't know what to make of this new life of yours. It's a good idea to talk with several different agents before you have one draw up your policies.

HOW ABOUT A LITERARY AGENT?

Over the course of your life, you've probably had experience with insurance agents and with real estate agents whose job it is to sell *you* something. In your new life, you may eventually want to use the services of a literary agent whose job it will be to sell something *for* you.

You'll find dozens of guides to literary agencies in your bookstore and long lists on the Internet as well. Many agents even have their own websites. That, in fact, is one of the problems. There are so many agents out there, it's tough to decide which one is best for you. One of the most effective ways to find one is to network with other writers to find out what their experience has been. It may even be helpful to have another writer recommend you to an agent, who will then be more willing to consider what you have to offer.

Of course, an agent doesn't work for free. The usual fee is 15 percent of the advance and future earnings on a book, but having a professional doing your negotiating for you will usually get you a better deal and even after paying the commission you may still be ahead of the game.

There are also agents who represent graphic artists and take on writers for clients as a sideline and will sell articles and other kinds of writing for you. Their fees are usually the same as those a literary agent charges and, just as literary agents share royalty income, they keep on earning commissions for as long as you continue working for a client they have found for you.

Your first contact with an agent will be through a query letter, selling your idea and your ability to pull it off. After that, the role is reversed and it is up to the agent to convince you that he or she can pull off the sale. Although most literary agents seem to have built walls around themselves—they won't take your phone calls if you haven't first exchanged letters—you do need to talk to them face-to-face before you sign a contract. You're going to become partners, at least for the term of the project, and for that you need personal rapport. Even if a dozen agents have turned down a chance to make money on your idea, don't jump into the lap of the first one who seems interested. Naturally, after two or three turndowns, you aren't in the mood to let a live one get away, but give it plenty of thought before you sign a contract. It isn't as though there aren't other agents waiting to hear from you. Besides, think how satisfying it can be to send off a rejection letter to somebody else.

One thing you should never do is to pay an agent a reading fee or a retainer upfront. They'll make enough money from your work after they invest a little work in it themselves.

Another way to get book ideas into print is by working with book packagers, who operate like movie producers. They start with an idea and develop it into a product which they sell either directly through a distributor or in partnership with a publisher. In most cases, book packagers assign ideas to writers and buy manuscripts on a "work-for-hire" basis, which means you do your job and get paid and that's the end of it. If this is your arrangement and your book becomes a best-seller, you won't collect any royalties. However, on the other hand, a good relationship with a packager can get you all the work you can handle.

CHAPTER SEVEN

Finding Work

After doing a series of arts and crafts books for a small publisher in San Francisco, Joni Prittie decided that she was ready for what she calls a "real" book and sent off a proposal to a New York publisher. Well one thing led to another, and before long Joni had an appointment to meet the editor at the publisher's booth at the American Booksellers Association Convention in the Jacob Javits center in New York City.

"I sent the proposal off on a Tuesday," she recalls, "and then began the angst of when to follow-up with a phone call. I didn't want to look too anxious, and I didn't want to seem inefficient, either. But it didn't matter. The editor called me on Friday afternoon. She said, 'Wow, yes, meet me next week at the American Booksellers Convention in New York.' Of course I showed up dressed in a great outfit with little brown shoes that matched my briefcase.

"I have a slight hearing problem in crowds, and I have to strain to catch all the words of a conversation, so I was a little uneasy when we sat down in that noisy convention center, she in her totally New York Saks yellow suit and I in my flowered skirt, white blouse, and those little brown shoes. She said, 'We can do a twenty-five K advance.' I said, 'Pardon me?' She said, 'All right, thirty.' Still not hearing, I said, 'Excuse me?' and she said, 'Okay, but thirty-five is our top and it is really all I can do.' By then I realized she was giving me figures for the advance on my book. I told her that thirty-five would be just fine. Negotiating by accident can be so much fun!"

Sandy Jones doesn't trust accidental luck. She took a course in negotiating, in fact, and it has more than paid for itself. "A third of the business of writing involves selling yourself, and you have to be able to take rejection in stride," she reports she's learned. "We're like T-shirt salesmen. Sometimes a hundred customers will look over what you have before one buys." Potential rejection notwithstanding, Sandy is a firm believer in never accepting the first offer. "When an editor makes an offer," she says, "I say it is less than I expected, and most often they will raise it. They'll even apologize." Among the things she learned in negotiating school is always to ask for a third more than you expect and then back down slowly. It never fails and, in her experience at least, she never has to back down by any amount close to a third.

Before you start looking for clients, you need to know what you're going to charge, but figuring out how much that should be involves a thicket of variables that can add up to a nightmare even for people who have been supporting themselves through their writing skills for decades.

Your neighborhood bookstore has it easy. Every book it stocks has a retail price printed on the jacket or cover. The manager knows what the store paid for it and how much the price can be discounted to make you think you're getting a bargain, but the people who write those books don't have such simple guidelines to help set their prices. More often than not, the publisher makes what seems to be "take-it-or-leave-it" offer, but as Joni and Sandy have both discovered, those offers aren't always quite what they seem. But you won't know unless you come back with a counteroffer. It is the same with every kind of writing. Still, especially when you are trying to get established, what is reasonable? You can't charge too much or you won't get any business; charge too little and you'll be out of business.

WHAT'S THE GOING RATE?

Pricing generally depends on what the traffic will bear in your market, and finding out what other writers charge for the kind of writing you expect to do is a good place to start. It's a touchy subject, though, because some people are uncomfortable discussing their earnings, even with close friends. Others may be less than candid when you ask them how much they earn, and the answer to the old question "Does she or doesn't she?" might well be "Only her accountant knows for sure."

Most writers are open and helpful, though, and rarely regard newcomers into their field as competition. Just be careful to ask only about their fees and not about their client list. They may volunteer the information anyway, because it is a long-standing tradition that writing is "a gentlemanly business." The idea that someone would even think of stealing business by cutting rates is as alien among writers as the probability of a doctor trolling another doctor's waiting rooms for patients.

When you survey other writers, though, keep in mind that style, skill, experience, and the nature of their clients are all factors that determine their rates. These are the same factors you also will be considering. And as much depends on where you sell your work as the time and effort that goes into it. If you have developed an understanding of the ins and outs of Social Security, for instance, *Modern Maturity* might pay you as much as three dollars per word for an article about it. The same piece would be worth less than a third of that to the *Wall Street Journal*.

CONSIDER STANDARD GUIDELINES

In its *Guide to Freelance Rates & Standard Practice*, available in most bookstores, the National Writers Union outlines fee structures in six markets for freelance writers from literary magazines to corporate communications. Its charts cover the range from low to high, and are based on averages. But they are a good starting point and, as the *Guide* points out, "consider your experience and clout, then aim as high on the scale as you can."

It's good advice, no matter which published pricing guide you turn to. There are dozens of them available and many of them are specific to the markets you may be considering, but before you buy one, the most important number you should check is the copyright date. Believe it or not, rates do change. They even go up sometimes. Arm yourself with the most recent information.

Even if you don't think you can reasonably charge the fees quoted in some of the published price lists, you can use them as a marketing tool among clients who feel obligated to pay the lowest possible price for your work. Many writers use the lists to prove that the fee they've set is within the ballpark. If you do that, though, browse through all the books in the bookstore's publishing section and buy the one that quotes the highest rates. That way, you'll be able to impress your client with proof that your rates are well below market averages.

Writer's Digest has a host of books available to answer questions you might have about selling your type of writing and what to charge for it. And the magazine that is the parent to all of them ought to be on your reading list as well. Other publications you'll find helpful and informative are *Freelance Success* (305/957-8857), *New Writer's Magazine* (813/953-7903), *Writer's Journal* (612/486-7818), and *Writer's Market* (800/289-0963). Who knows? Once your business is up and running, any or all of them represents a market for your writing.

LET THE CLIENT BE YOUR GUIDE

The last item in your pricing survey is your potential clients, but that may be the trickiest of all to determine. Ask anyone what they expect to pay for the things they're hiring you to write and the answer is sure to be "as little as possible." On the other hand, most businesses work with budgets, and if you get close enough to a client, you might be able to find out how much has been budgeted for a particular job. Remember, before you sign a contract, you should negotiate. Most budgets have air built into them.

WHAT DO YOU NEED TO EARN?

Carl Nelson, a freelance advertising writer in the Baltimore area, says that "a good rule of thumb in setting rates is that you will rarely be able to bill more than twelve hundred hours a year in this field—about three days a week. The rest gets eaten up by meetings, billing, play time, and so on. You don't get rich, but you can make a decent living. I will write anything for anyone for seventy-five dollars an hour. I'm fifty-six years old and have cut back to an average of two days a week, but I still earn sixty thousand dollars a year. I tell people that I have the best part-time job in America."

Your plans may be to have America's best full-time business, and as a freelance writer you're on the right track, but, like your clients, your business should be working with a budget, and you need to do a little pencil-pushing before you agree to any price for a writing assignment. Thanks to that business plan you put together, you know what it's costing you to deliver the goods. You know what it is taking to keep your business running, from the electric and phone bills to the grocery bill. Add it all up and it will give you a good idea what you need to earn in a month to keep body and soul together.

You can plan on working a lot of overtime and giving up your weekends, but for all practical purposes, you have twenty working days in a month and, at eight hours a day, that adds up to one hundred sixty hours. But, as Carl Nelson points out, a lot of that time is going to be spent selling and delivering jobs among other things. And you'll be invited to meetings where you're the only person in the room who isn't collecting a paycheck for being there. It's reasonable to assume, following Carl's formula, that would leave you with less than a hundred hours a month to make money. Possibly you're not planning to work in the meeting-intensive advertising business, but even homebodies among freelance writers can't count on more than a hundred twenty hours of actual productive time in a given month. Determine which number is closest to your situation, and divide your costs by it. It will give you a good idea of what you should be charging for an hour of your time just to break even. Most service businesses mark up that basic figure, which they call "direct labor," somewhere between 50 and 100 percent, and so should you, to be sure you're making a profit.

Sometimes you may have to settle for less, to be sure, especially when you're establishing yourself, but make that basic hourly rate your goal and it will take a lot of the guesswork out the pricing dilemma.

CONSIDER THE VARIABLES

While you're pushing that pencil, go a step further to factor in some of the variables all writers deal with. You'll have jobs that will have to be changed after you considered them finished. Many writers allow for that in their original contract by adding a clause specifying a charge for rewriting. It is an absolute must in cases where the client makes changes from the original concept, but, in general, even minor second thoughts will take time to incorporate into your text, and from now on your time is money.

Some clients also will take their own sweet time before sending you a check. Although most freelance writers say they are usually paid for their work within a month of rendering a bill, some large publishers or advertising agencies may consider forty-five days perfectly fine. And remember, too, that their accounting departments won't even think about you until a job has been written and accepted, not to mention a bill submitted and sub-jected to a round of approvals.

Don't forget, too, that there will be seasonal cycles in your business and there are going to be months where you won't have enough work to keep you busy for one hundred twenty hours. Of course, you'll also have some months when there aren't enough hours to get it all done. However, don't count on the times when you have to burn the midnight oil to even things out. If you were working for someone other than yourself, you'd expect to be paid extra for overtime, wouldn't you?

WATCH OUT FOR NEGATIVE CASH FLOW

If your plan for the future involves selling articles to magazines, you need to know that there is a difference between making a sale and seeing your name at the top of a printed article. Some magazines won't pay you until your piece is actually published. If you are writing for a quarterly with that kind of policy, and your story is held out of the next issue, you may have to wait six months for your money. It happens.

Magazine and newspaper publishers often allow for a kill fee, usually a quarter of the accepted price, in their contracts. Most writers skim over that clause because it's inconceivable to them that the article they proposed and sold won't make it into print. But that happens, too, sometimes because another publication has scooped your client on the story that you researched and sold. Once in a while an article may be below an editor's standards, but in that case you should be given a chance to bring it up to snuff and not settle for twenty-five cents on the dollar. Be sure that the contract gives you that opportunity, and while you're going over that part, ask if the kill fee percentage can be raised. You'll be surprised how often it can.

If you hired a contractor to build you a house and then decided you didn't like it when it was finished or thought it looked too much like the house next door, what do you suppose he'd say if you told him you weren't moving in—and in that case, you were only going to pay 25 percent of the price? You'd probably find yourself in court, and losing the case.

In most kinds of writing, from books to promotion pieces, you are usually expected to pay your own expenses for travel and phone calls and other out-of-pocket costs, but most magazine and newspaper publishers are willing to reimburse you for them, as long as you're careful to be sure it's spelled out in your contract. Be sure, as well, that the contract spells out what the publisher will consider reasonable expenses and how long it will take for you to get your money back.

Your contract for a magazine or newspaper article will also spell out who will get the leftovers—that is, reprint rights after it has been published the first time. These days, controversy is raging over electronic rights, and the dust there won't settle for a long time to come. Most book publishers as well as periodical publishers try to retain those rights for themselves, but it is in your best interest to balk when they do.

The copyright for any material you write belongs to you unless you sign it away. Don't. Bill Allen never does. He routinely resells magazine articles he's written to other publications and he finds that publishers will usually change their contracts to give him the rights when he asks them to. "You're not going to sell every story again," he says, "but I've been able to add a lot to my income by selling previously published material to syndicates, in-house corporate magazines, and even *Readers' Digest*." Jim has been so successful at it, in fact, that when a publication makes him an offer to reprint one of his stories, he often holds back hoping someone else will make a better one. Sometimes he finds the original bid will go up after he plays hard to get.

Always keep in mind that publishers have more money than you do. Never, ever agree to any clause in a contract that might allow them to take money out of your pocket.

HOW WILL YOU CHARGE?

The hourly rate you establish for yourself will be the basis for what you're charging for most jobs, though more often than not freelance writers come up with a bottom-line figure that reflects the amount of time they think it will take them to finish the job.

John Larson, who runs a boutique ad agency in Chicago, has seen his average hourly rate for trade jobs double from thirty to sixty dollars since he started out in the early 1980s. His retail rate, for one-time clients, is twice as high. "I charge by the project," he says, "because that way a client knows up-front what it is going to cost. But I bill by the hour if they request revisions.

"Before you quote a price, there are a few questions you need to ask yourself: Are your clients small businesses or big corporations? Is it a one-time job? Or is there repeat business that can make you comfortable with a lower hourly rate?

"After taking those things into account, I recommend that you shouldn't be either the cheapest or the most expensive. Instead, make yourself the best value for your client's investment."

Some of your clients are going to invite you to meetings, and some of the time you're going to find that it takes them a lot of time to get to the point. There is office gossip to be rehashed, of course, and there will be participants with their own axes to grind that have little or nothing to do with the subject at hand.

Even meetings that are run efficiently take a big chunk out of your workday with travel to and from the client's office. And when was the last time you went to a meeting that started on time?

These are all things that you need to consider when you set your fee and probably the best way to do it is by quoting a flat hourly rate, but you'll find that the majority of clients will want you to start out with a bottom-line figure so that they can build it into their budgets. Obviously you can't plan for long unproductive meetings with first-time clients, but it's a good idea to factor in for the possibility. Again, keep in mind that everyone else in that conference room will be picking a paycheck at the end of the week and your time is every bit as valuable as theirs.

But no matter whether you charge by the hour or by the job, any price you quote should be not so much for the job itself but for the results it will bring, and you should make that your top priority when you sit down with a prospective client. Remember the old salesman's rule: "Sell the sizzle, not the steak."

ALWAYS HAVE A CONTRACT

Any price you quote is etched in stone. If it takes you longer than you thought it would to get a job done, you can't go back and bump up the price, but sometimes the extra time comes from changes your client makes along the way, which is another good reason to have a contract before you start—even a simple letter agreement is better than nothing. The point is to get it in writing.

Most publishers get the point, and if you're selling a book or an article, they'll give you a contract to countersign before you start. But don't sign it until you've read it. All contracts may look alike, even to someone like you whose life revolves around words, but they're not all the same and they are not binding until both you and the publisher have signed them. Before you do put your signature on the document be sure all your needs are addressed. This is an agreement, not a mandate. If you think the numbers need some massaging, don't be afraid to ask. If your relationship with a publisher has reached the point of asking for your signature, you're probably not going to lose the opportunity just because you asked for a better deal. And you'll be getting terms *you* want, not what someone else has decided for you.

If you are writing foundation grant requests, training manuals, promotion materials, or any of the other thousands of projects freelance writers are asked to do, write your own contract. You have a good idea what you need and what you want and it should be spelled out in advance. The client may negotiate some of the points you make, but by the time you start the job both of you will know exactly what to expect of one another.

MAKING IT WORK

You've probably already given some thought about where you're going to find business—maybe it's a former employer who has said the company can use your help.

Jim McClure started his freelance business working for the corporation that had just given him a buyout, but Jim was lucky. Because of the tax laws, companies can't downsize by offering buyout packages and then go on using the ex-employee as an independent contractor. In Jim's case, the arrangement worked because the assignments he does now is for a subsidiary company within the corporation and not the division he worked for as full-time employee. More important, this company is just one of a big portfolio of clients that Jim services. He didn't spread himself around to satisfy an IRS rule, he follows a rule that applies to every freelance writer in America: having just one or two clients, no matter how big or how promising they are, is like building a house on sand.

As accountant Irwin Fenishel puts it, "concentration of risk, a small customer base, is something banks take a very dim view of and any small business owner needs to avoid like the plague." No matter what your view of banks may be, that policy is right on the money, and if you expect this new business of yours to support you for the rest of your life, don't ever put all your eggs in one basket. The small business world abounds with stories of businesses that have failed by relying too heavily on a couple of key clients, no matter how tempting or promising they seemed.

That said, one of the keys to starting any new business is to build it a buck at a time, and that means keeping your client family small at the beginning. You might have clients lined up waiting for you to declare your independence. You know you're a better writer than the rest of the pack, and you're raring to go. In spite of all that, you should still move at a measured pace. At the very least, it will give you time to get used to life on your own, and to try different kinds of writing. You never know, this move you're making might mean more than just a change in your lifestyle, it may be a change in your writing style as well.

FINDING BUSINESS

Ask a freelance writer about where business leads come from, and the answer most often will be, "Word of mouth." All through the life of your business, satisfied clients are going to be your best source of new accounts, but when you're starting out, you're going to need more than referrals. You'll need to get the word out to people who need your services but don't know you or anyone else you've ever worked with. To accomplish that, you should develop a marketing plan that will help lead you to your prospects.

Marketing plans are second nature to most big companies, and most of them are matters of life and death. In your former life, you may even have been involved in writing them. This time, though, it's your life you're planning and that's a whole lot more important. The same resources big companies use are available to you and you can use them in the same way. It all begins by asking yourself who needs your services and who your targets should be.

When Clay Morgan sold his first article to a martial arts magazine while he was still in high school, he knew he wouldn't be happy doing anything but writing. Although he is an expert in the martial arts field, he had to broaden his market. A reference book he found in the local library called *Bacon's Media Guide, Magazine Edition,* turned out to be a gold mine. He writes for a broad range of magazines today, and his biggest account is *Furrow Farming,* whose editor doesn't know, and probably doesn't care, that Clay's second business is running a judo training school. Over the years, he has found that magazines that have corporate sponsors tend to pay higher rates, and these days he makes those his prime targets.

The way professional marketers begin to find their targets is by studying statistics, beginning with those they call demographics. This is simply a study of where people live, how they make their living, and what their lifestyle is like. The numbers, and names, that apply to your business community are usually available at the local library or through the chamber of commerce or some similar business organization. A surprising number of these groups may have a need for someone like you to write flyers and brochures, business plans, and proposals. Don't forget that simple jobs like these can do wonders for your cash flow. By the way, your demographic research can also provide a rich source of ideas for articles and stories.

Even better is the second set of statistics professional marketers treasure—called psychographics—which give clues about what makes people buy one product or service over another. Using surveys and focus groups, large organizations get clues that help them come up with what the advertising community calls a "unique selling proposition," the plan that helps set their products apart from the competition and turn prospects into loyal customers.

Small business people like you don't have the resources to retain high-priced marketing consultants to help them arrive at such conclusions, but you don't really need them either. Because your business will be small at the beginning, you'll be in closer contact with editors and others who hire you to write for them. Every meeting with a client should be a mini-focus group. Keep your ears open, and you'll learn something more than just the details of the job at hand. Listen to enough of them, and you'll know what you're doing right. Next lead with those strengths in the proposals, and anything else that come out of your marketing plan aimed at building new business.

BUILDING A BRAND

Identifying potential clients is only half the battle when you put together a marketing plan. The other half, targeting and reaching them, may be even more important.

As a writer, the way you put words together is as unique to you as the shape of your nose, but don't expect a potential client to notice that. Your writing style is not as plain as the nose on your face, except to you, and no one will know how good you really are unless you make it a point to tell them.

Calling attention to your style and to your approach can make all the difference in a client's decision as to whether to hire you or someone else with a similar idea. Yes, you need to start with an idea, but ideas are only as good as what you propose to do with them.

Build an image for yourself and the client's decision will be easy. Eventually, it may become more important than what you charge, and it could help open the door to higher fees. The bottom line may be important when a client makes a decision to buy one writer's work over another's, but in the end it's what they perceive they will be getting for their money that is most important of all.

Keep in mind that even though your ultimate product is words on a piece of paper, what you're actually selling is what those words can do for the people who are going to pay you to put them together. An ad, a newsletter, a direct-mail piece, a magazine article, a grant request, and even a book generally have one purpose: to attract attention that results in sales for your client. As Walter Camp, one of the pioneers of the motivation business, once pointed out, "Nothing happens, not a wheel turns, until first a cash register rings."

CREATE A PORTFOLIO

Mark Stock, who packages marketing plans for shopping malls in the Atlanta area, usually carries photocopies of his work that he leaves behind when he makes a sales call, but he also has a full-blown portfolio in the trunk of his car just in case a prospect wants to see more. They rarely do. "I go into the trunk more often for a jack than for that book," he reports. Jeffrey has also developed his own website, but he doesn't put samples of his work there. "I use it to display testimonials from clients," he says, "and I've found several new clients among people who discovered me on the Internet."

Kelle Larkin added to her base of writing articles for a local newspaper in Michigan with a monthly column for a magazine in New England, which she discovered browsing the Internet. Like Jeffrey, Kelle also has her own website, and she posts writing samples there. It is her only portfolio, and she's happy to report it does its job very well.

No matter where you get your sales leads, there will be times when you'll have to meet face-to-face with potential clients before you get the job. And you can't depend on a firm handshake or a wink and a smile to get the job for you. When you do make a sales call, take along a selection of work you've produced and make it as close as possible to what your prospect is looking for. You probably don't need a fancy leather carrying case and, like Mark Stock, you may find that a small selection of carefully chosen photocopies will be enough.

Be careful to do some research before you start gathering samples. If the assignment is coming from an advertising agency with an automotive account, the creative director is going to want to see what you've done for other carmakers, and will usually regard anything else as irrelevant. But what if (you have every right to ask) you've never written about cars? What if, for that matter, this is your first sales call and you're hoping it will get you your first job?

Of course you have to be honest about it, but until you have built a collection of specific samples to show, consider putting together some pages that will show what you *can* do. Although many people have a built-in prejudice against looking at samples that haven't been gussied up with illustrations, you are in the word business, after all, and in the end that is what they ought to be looking at anyway.

In many cases, getting samples of printed jobs can be as difficult as getting the job itself. Clay Morgan found that this is a frustration with the small businesses he works with, but he solved the problem by putting it in his contracts that along with prompt payment, he also requires six samples of the work itself. Bill Allen points out that most magazine contracts agree to forward full copies or tear sheets, but some editors forget every now and then, and he makes it a policy to buy copies when a magazine hits the newsstands.

If you regularly check newspaper classifieds for freelance opportunities (and you should), you'll find that most ask for printed samples along with a résumé. That's a good way to run out of samples, but most writers report that photocopies will do the job—and often get the job. Just be careful that the quality of the photocopy is as good as the quality of your writing.

Some beginning writers agree to write on speculation to show a prospective client how they might handle a specific job. You may enjoy writing very much and don't mind putting a little effort into providing free samples. But in the end, it probably isn't a very good idea. Who's going to pay the rent while you're working on it? Many people who write articles operate on the theory that they have to do the research before they write a query anyway, and they might as well write the piece, too, while they're at it and then go for the sale. That's fine if you're independently wealthy, but it is much better, and easier too, to send off outlines that will make the sale before you do the work. Your landlord will be grateful if you do.

Your portfolio will grow as your business does, of course, and the time will come when you can adjust it to the specific needs of a prospect. As you go along, you'll also gather testimonials and these ought to become an integral part of your portfolio. Nothing can sell your words quite as effectively as someone else's words of praise.

IT MAY PAY TO ADVERTISE

When you're putting together your marketing plan, the advertising salespeople at local newspapers and magazines, radio, and television stations are a prime source of information about the local business community. All of them have media kits which are filled with information about the people they reach and much of it can be priceless in your quest to determine the people you should be reaching, too.

Clay Morgan discovered early that "most ad agencies won't bother with small businesses, and there are a lot of them here in Memphis. I fill that gap." In some cases, he finds those small

clients through media reps who are eager for the business themselves and are pleased to recommend him.

In general, freelance writers—even the ones who write advertising copy—don't advertise. Many do, however, list their names
and their specialties on one or more of the several job-search
sites on the Internet. You can find them with the keyword "freelance writers." There is usually no charge to add your listing,
and although it isn't a sure thing, there are opportunities there.
Clay Morgan says, "I have eight steady clients who have found
me that way."

SELLING BY MAIL

Not every sales call you make is going to get business for you.
At least not right now. But that doesn't mean it won't pay off
somewhere down the road, as long as you keep in touch.

Jim McClure, who uses his experience in crisis management
as one of the aspects of his freelance public relations business,
routinely sends letters to executives whose promotions have been
announced in the business press. "It's a simple letter that invites
them to 'think of me if you get in a crunch,' and it works."

Beth D'Addono is pleased to report that "The current PR
writing job I have, one or two days a week at a $250 day rate,
I got from a direct mailing I sent out. I mailed twenty letters to
prospects I hadn't heard from in a while and got eight responses.
One turned into this job."

As anyone in the direct-mail business will tell you, that is an
almost unheard-of response rate. But Beth says that in addition
to the fact that it was "a great letter," it also went to people who
knew her but needed to be reminded of her availability and her
interest. If you don't believe in the axiom "out of sight, out
mind" yet, you'll come to understand what it means when you
start your writing business.

Among the prospects who respond to your reminders that you

are still alive and kicking, some are going to say, "Thanks, but no thanks," but that doesn't mean you've lost them forever. Save their names in your computer and keep in touch with them. Maybe you'll produce a job down the road that would be useful to them. When you do, send them a copy with a short note saying that you thought they'd be interested. They very well might be.

FREE ADVERTISING

One of these days you're going to bump into a prospect on the street or in the checkout line at the supermarket. It will be someone you worked with before or a friend who promised to send work your way but has neglected to since you started your own business. "I've been meaning to call you," the person will gush. Then you'll exchange business cards and you may wind up with a job you hadn't expected.

That person, by the way, might have called long ago if you had sent a letter to all your friends, acquaintances, and former associates telling them about your new business. It doesn't have to be an out-and-out solicitation, but a subtle suggestion that you might be offering a service they can use.

Suppose you hadn't been on that street corner at that precise moment or decided to put off the grocery shopping, do you think they'd have called you? Probably not. But you can't be everywhere, and you can't expect to bump into business every time you decide to take a walk in the park. (However, never leave home without a supply of business cards.)

After building a steady business as a book editor by charging a flat fee that included unlimited follow-ups to help writers market their books, Kimberly Rufer-Bach went through a long slow period with no new clients. "I went to work in a pizza parlor," she recalls, "and I thought that was the end of my literary career. But old clients found me there, and I went back to work with them by popular demand." However, don't expect to meet with Kimberly's success yourself. It is rare for clients to come calling unless you do something to nudge them first.

PRESS RELEASES

There are a few ways you can keep your name out there, even when your face is glued to a computer screen. One of them is to send out press releases to local newspapers and to trade papers in your field. You should do it when you start up, of course, but also when you sign a new contract. If you are writing a book, don't rely on the publisher to let the world know about it, do it for yourself. When the book appears in a catalog, send out a press release to publications you believe are read by bookstore owners. It will pave the way for you when you show up in their store to pull copies of your book out from the back of the shelf.

As a writer, you may have become an expert on a particular topic, but even if you write extensively about it, nobody will connect you with your expertise unless you point it out to them. Get to know reporters who also write about that subject and encourage them to put your name on their Rolodexes for consulting (and quoting) on new developments. Once they get to know you, they'll call you. And they'll use your name in the stories they write. That, of course, will add to your credibility with the things you are writing yourself.

USE BROADCASTERS

Broadcast personalities also manage to come up with "experts" to comment on the things they're reporting, and if your niche makes you an expert on a particular subject, as it often does, you should make them aware of it. There is no magic involved.

Producers keep files of contacts in every imaginable field and when they need an expert they just pick up the phone. It all begins for you when you answer the phone and find a producer who will interview you. Once you've done that, though, you may still have to wait a while for your big break. That's show business.

GO FOR AWARDS

You should also make it a point to submit your writing in every competition you can (or, even better, get your clients to do it for you). Advertising agencies thrive on the awards they've gathered, and so do journalists—did you know you can nominate *yourself* for a Pulitzer Prize?

Movie stars, screenwriters, and producers often command higher fees and get promotional value out of being "nominated for an Academy Award," even if they've never won one. Even an "honorable mention" can go a long way in enhancing your prestige and your value to a publisher. And you don't have to enter national competitions to make a good impression. Recognition from the local chamber of commerce, a regional trade association, or the ad club is going to get your name in the papers and deserves a place on your résumé as well as in your portfolio.

SELL YOURSELF

Everybody knows that a customer who is pleased with your work will be a repeat customer. But keeping a client satisfied goes beyond delivering award-winning work. As the old song says, "It Ain't What You Do, It's the Way That You Do it."

The most important thing you can do is make your clients feel important. That may seem too obvious to mention, but the business world is a lot less personal today than it once was, and old-fashioned courtesy seems to have become just that: an old-fashioned idea. However, you can easily turn that into an advantage. In a world where there is so little of it, simple courtesy can stand out like a summer sunrise. It doesn't take any effort, and it doesn't cost anything. Just a simple "thank you" for the business can work wonders.

A friendly attitude can go a long way with everyone you deal with. When you visit a client's office, don't run past the receptionist without stopping to chat for a minute or so. It's a trick that stands many newspaper reporters in good stead. Sometimes they find that they can get more information from the outer office than from the inner sanctum, but it is also a gesture that will be remembered when the time comes that you have to interrupt a client's meeting for a phone call that can't wait.

The fact is, everybody in an office you visit is as important as the person you've gone there to see. For one thing, some of those people are going to be promoted one of these days, and others are going to move on to different companies. Make sure they'll remember you.

NETWORK YOUR WAY TO NEW BUSINESS

Establishing a network simply means keeping in touch with old friends and associates as often as you can. It also means making new contacts by meeting people face-to-face whenever possible. Nobody will go to a stranger when they already know someone who can deliver an article, a brochure, or a book when they want one.

Beth D'Addono says that follow-up is the most important part of networking. "When I get a business card at a party, I call and send stuff without fail. I make it a point to talk to everybody, but I'm not pushy. I get some contacts on press trips I go on, meet editors and hear about things they are planning. And I *always* follow-up."

Even if some of the people you meet may never need you to write anything for them, it is a good bet that if you make the right impression they'll be your biggest booster among friends who might. People take great pleasure in recommending sources to friends. "Hey, I know someone who would be perfect to write that for you," is one of the friendliest statements there is because it connects friends who might otherwise have remained strangers. And sometimes it is surprising where big, profitable jobs actually come from.

DEVELOP CENTERS OF INFLUENCE

At some point in your life, maybe when you got married or promoted in your job, you probably had a call from a life insurance agent. When you finally agreed to listen to the sales pitch, you may have discovered that your best friend sicked him on you. Then, as you signed on the dotted line, the agent asked you if you had any other friends who might need coverage. Of course you did, and the agent had some new leads. That technique, called "centers of influence," has sold billions of dollars' worth of life insurance over the years, and it still works. It's another form of networking.

It can work wonders for you, too. If a client praises you work, don't be a shrinking violet. Ask for a letter you can put in your portfolio, then ask for the name of someone else who should know what you can do. Either approach might get you your next job.

People in today's business world—and it is especially true in publishing and in advertising—are likely to have worked for several different companies before landing at the desk where you caught up with them. They often know other people with needs similar to theirs, and they don't usually mind sharing sources with them. As you get to know your clients, you'll get a feel for who might be help you and who not, but chances are you're going to find a lot more of the former than the latter.

BE A JOINER

Over most of the country's history, professional salespeople measured their success by the number of organizations they belonged to. They may not have called it networking, but they all regarded it as the best way to make customers out of strangers.

When she moved from New York to Colorado, Debra Jason made it a point to join as many organizations as she had time for, from the local chamber of commerce to the Rocky Mountain Direct Marketing Association, of which she became president. But, she says, "joining isn't enough. You have to get involved. I write articles for organization newsletters and, recently, when I gave a speech at a chamber of commerce meeting one of the members asked me to repeat it for his sales staff, and I earned a nice fee." And where do you think that member started turning to have his sales promotion materials written?

Most writers who belong to professional and business organizations find the networking opportunities priceless, and not always for the business it produces. Beth Smollin, a New Jersey technical writer, says, "I find writing to be a very lonely job, and I make it a point to get out of the house as often as I can to recharge my batteries. When I first started, I usually panicked every time something new or different came along and I was spending too much time wandering around and putting it off. Then I discovered a local service organization that has weekly lunch meetings. I thought I was wasting too much time as it was, so I put off joining that, too. But then I realized that by giving some purpose to my wandering around, another part of my brain was actually working out the problem. I don't go crazy anymore."

In the end, whether you become a joiner or not depends on the business you need to target, the kinds of organizations available in your area, and your own personality. For many, it makes good sense to join local business groups that are likely to have potential clients among their membership. And if there are any in your area, joining professional associations can help you share ideas as well as frustrations with others who are in the same boat as you.

You'll also meet a lot of people, and make good contacts, by joining sales and marketing groups and signing up for their seminars. In your new life, you are going to be in the sales business, too, and there is no reason why you shouldn't be as professional at it as you are with your writing.

TRY VOLUNTEERING

Another option you might consider is to volunteer some time at such institutions as the local library. This will instantly connect you with others from your community and you might be surprised who *else* is volunteering. Just give careful thought to the kinds of organizations you want to support.

Be leery, too, about volunteering too much of your service as a writer. Thanks to desktop computers, even block associations have newsletters these days, and your forays into pro-bono work can easily get out of hand. To be sure, it's a good way to showcase your work and to produce samples for your portfolio that will impress clients, but it's possible to carry altruism too far. Be careful that you don't find yourself spending more time than you intended producing work that you aren't going to be paid for.

Keep in mind that some people will think that because you

are at home every day playing around with a computer that you are either retired or independently wealthy. Tell them that you are a professional writer, and their image will be of TV's Jessica Fletcher flitting around with unlimited time to track down murderers; or of Hemingway, with enough time on his hands to spend months on safari. You know better, but they might not.

KEEP UP WITH YOUR FIELD

A few years ago, a study reported in *Journalism Quarterly* suggested that many freelance writers were courting endangered species status by not keeping up with the latest technology. The research concluded that unless freelance writers caught up with staff writers who were using faxes, E-mail, and computers, they'd be "swept off the playing field."

That was then and this is now, and such a warning today is like telling a farmer that he'll face bankruptcy if he doesn't get a tractor. Virtually all freelance writers have caught up with technology by now, but keeping on top of it is still important—and not just with the tools of your trade.

No matter what your niche, you need to keep up-to-the-minute, and that means lots of browsing in bookstores and on the Internet, not just to research the job at hand, but to keep your eye on the future.

Remember that when all is said and done, you are in the information business, and the only way to succeed is to keep yourself informed. It is what your competition will be doing, and what your clients will expect of you.

They'll also expect you to be equipped with the things they consider basic that may not have seemed so important a few years ago, like E-mail access. Back in the mid-1970s, a study conducted for corporate purchasing agents concluded that although fax machines were "useful in libraries and newspaper offices, they do not have applications in the business world." Of course, that was a long time ago, but it demonstrates the danger of making assumptions. If your word processing program isn't up-to-date, it doesn't matter that it still serves all your needs; more important is the question of whether your clients are going to have trouble opening your documents. You need to anticipate problems like that, and the only way to do it is by keeping yourself informed.

CHAPTER EIGHT

Do I Have a Business?

Once the start-up phase of your freelance writing business and its day-to-day operation has become routine, step back and take a look at how your life has changed. Taking inventory is crucial to seeing what works, what doesn't, and how you might do things differently to improve your new life. Sometimes the most obvious things are difficult to see when you're racing toward a deadline.

AM I FINDING THE SATISFACTION I HOPED FOR?

Satisfaction is a goal—and it can be an elusive one at the start of any new business. There are few businesses out there that don't experience any hardship whatsoever, so consider it part of the package of your new venture.

It may be possible that you've become disenchanted because you are overwhelmed with work and don't see any end to it. It may be that the work that has become your niche takes more time than you anticipated. If that is the case, you may be able to get around the problem by shifting your focus.

Many successful freelance writers find there is more demand for what they do than there are hours in their days, but most make it a point not to take on more work than they think they can handle. It isn't easy to say "no" to a job offer, but remember that you are in business for the long haul. There are probably more offers where that particular one came from, and they'll come at times when you can more comfortably fit them into your schedule.

Remember, too, that when you have more work than you can comfortably handle, the quality of your writing will suffer because of the pressure. Your reputation is your number-one asset, and you need to hand in your best work for every job you take on.

If long, unrewarding hours are standing between you and happiness, try to schedule small vacations every now and then. A long weekend away from your computer can work wonders in restoring your energy and your enthusiasm. Yes, the meter stops when you go away and you not only won't be earning any money for a couple of days, but you'll be spending it instead. However, it was a heavy workload that painted you into this corner, and R&R is the secret way out.

Elizabeth Judd has learned that taking it easy once in awhile is the best antidote to pressure, but what she hasn't learned, she says, is how to sell herself. "I don't love every job I take on," she admits, "and I rely too much on having job offers come to me. If I were more aggressive about it, I know I'd have the luxury of being able to turn down work I'd rather not be bothered with." This is something to keep in mind if you find yourself spending too many dull, unrewarding days.

If procrastination leads to a backlog of work, consider scheduling your more tiresome jobs at a specific time early in the day to get them out of the way. It will give you a chance to look forward to the work that you have the rest of the afternoon.

Sometimes tiny changes can have a big impact on a small business. You've come a long way in this business of yours, so if things don't seem to be working right, fight hard to come up with creative answers. If you are really stumped, try networking with other writers. Carl Nelson points out that "like most others in this business, I have been helped by someone in the past. I can remember pathetic looks from creative directors who stooped to tell me how to put an idea portfolio together. 'Tear out a bad ad and do it right; tear out a good ad and do the next in the series. Demonstrate that you can do this job.' Because none of us would be where we are without someone's help, most of us are willing to try to repay the favor."

AM I MAKING OR LOSING MONEY?

Knowing whether you're making or losing money isn't always easy in a business like freelance writing because the biggest commodity you are dealing with is time, and that doesn't lend itself to a balance sheet comparing money you've spent to money you've earned.

Most freelance writers don't seem to have a clue about how much money they're making until their accountant puts the numbers together at tax time. Sometimes it's a pleasant surprise, sometimes not. You're often too busy making money to keep track of it. For the most part, making it to the end of the month with enough to pay the bills seems to be all that matters, but your living expenses and your company's overhead can get out of hand if you're not careful.

Just about every small business has cash-flow problems at one time or another, and freelance writers certainly aren't immune to them. After you've been in your own business for awhile, you may notice that bill collecting is a big part of your job, even if it wasn't in your original job description. Sometimes the question isn't whether you're making or losing money, but when are those checks going to arrive? Then there are times when your receivables don't match your expenses, and at times like that you need to make a realistic appraisal of your future as a freelance writer and whether you can afford to be one.

Fortunately, many freelance writers don't seem to have collection problems. Most say they can count on being paid within a month of billing, except for the corporate clients who take a bit longer. Be aware that you may get a client who goes out of business or overspends on a project and leaves you without a check at the end. Such things usually happen when you can least afford them. Your only recourse is to take the client to court, but that could cost more than the amount you're owed, and you'd still have to wait months to actually collect what's owed to you. Or you can just lick your wounds. Either way, the time lost is usually more important than the money. You're going to find yourself running in place to catch up. There probably isn't any way to avoid a problem like that except to try to find out everything you can about a new client's track record before you start a job. It may take more time than you care to invest, but consider the alternative, particularly for a large job.

IS IT TIME TO MODIFY MY ORIGINAL PLAN?

If, after time, you find that your business isn't producing as much income, or as much satisfaction, as you had hoped, the solution may be to use your skills in a different way.

Karen Gravelle has established a very profitable niche for herself as an authority on AIDS research, and there is almost no limit to the technical writing jobs she can get from pharmaceutical firms. Better still, she loves the work. But, she backs away from it occasionally. "I have a short attention span," she reveals, "and I get just as much satisfaction, although certainly not as much money, writing children's books."

Then, not too long ago, Karen discovered a new way to use her expertise. "A client called and asked me to come into his office," she recalls, "and we were three-quarters into the meeting before I realized he was talking about an industrial film and not an information booklet. I didn't give him a clue that I'd never done a film before, and accepted the assignment. When I got home I called a friend who does write films and asked to see some scripts. I'm telling you, if the average chambermaid knew how easy it is to write them, we'd all be making our own beds in hotels. I do more film than print work now, and I love the paychecks."

Karen's core business wasn't showing any signs of tapering off, but she was pleased to have found a way to make more money with less effort. In many cases, though, writers find their original sources dropping away and their income dropping, too. Sometimes the work may become repetitive and less satisfying, and when it does, that may be a sign that you should be looking for fresh challenges. No matter how promising or satisfying a business may seem at the beginning, you may find after time that it's a good idea to cut your losses and move on to Plan B. It isn't a sign of failure, but rather a realistic approach to improving your life.

DO I SEE A BRIGHT FUTURE?

If you aren't finding the income you were expecting, or the satisfaction, analyze the possibilities of making the future brighter. It took a lot of faith and courage to start up your own business in the first place and the same qualities that kept you going then can help you turn it in the right direction.

No business enterprise is a sure thing, but thousands have discovered that, in terms of controlling your own destiny, being a freelance writer is as good as it gets. There are potholes along the way, but with foresight most of the deep ones can be avoided.

If a major client suddenly goes out of business, hopefully you've been cultivating options along the way. If you foresee competition mushrooming all around you, be ready to alter your plan and develop a new specialty. One of the beauties of a freelance writing business is that there are so many specialties to choose from.

The future never takes care of itself in anybody's life, but when all is said and done, if you keep an eye on it and plan for it, your future as a freelance writer can be brighter than you imagined.

YOU NEVER STOP LEARNING

One of writing's real joys is the number of things you learn along the way. No other profession offers so many opportunities to explore a changing world, and to dig into its past. No matter what kind of writing you plan to do, whether it be advertising copy, technical manuals, personality profiles, or even the Great American Novel, you'll learn something new with every page.

Get ready to have fun making a living for a change. If you're like most people who have found a second life as a freelance writer, you're going to find yourself looking back someday and asking yourself, "Why didn't I do this sooner?"

Monday Morning Pep Talks

Inspiration to Make Your Week THRIVE

Colene H. Elridge

DEDICATION

For my Mom, Claudia, for doing it all, even when it was hard. You taught me how to persevere, and I would not be the woman I am without your love and support.

"You can change the world, or you can change a world. Both are equally as important."

CONTENTS

ACKNOWLEDGMENTS

So many people to thank! My brother, Colmon for always believing in me. You're the best brother a girl could ask for! My brother from another mother, and best friend, Keith for being my Gayle, for always supporting my crazy dreams, and just being the best ever. My amazing husband, Robert. You cheer me on, you let me whine, you are my constant 5 that's always calm, you cuddle best! I love you! To Debra Locker, for being incredibly patience and being the best PR woman I know. To the Committee of NTOO... we got us! To Beau for being love in human form. To all my family and friends who had to put up with my crazy time putting this book together, you are amazing! To the bees, for teaching me that we can all defy the odds! And to each and every Monday Morning Pep Talk reader... y'all are awesome and constantly inspire me!

FOREWORD

You know those people that you meet for the first time and you just know your life is going to be better for having known them? That is Colene Elridge.

I was first introduced to Colene through a mutual friend and client of mine who introduced us because, well, "we just had to know each other."

And she was right.

A chat with Colene is like balm for your soul.

She's a breath of fresh air.
She's a warm blanket when you're cold.
And she's a belly laugh when you're feeling blue.

Every time I think of Colene, I can't help but smile because her energy is so infectious.

Lucky for me, I get to enjoy that energy in person over a cup of coffee or some chips and queso, but if you haven't had the pleasure of spending time with

Colene in-person, well, lucky for you, she's put decades of wisdom into her incredible new book.

This book, Monday Morning Pep Talks, means you have access to Colene's magic whenever you need it.

Colene's gift for breaking down complex topics into relatable stories, and for knowing exactly what you need to hear when you need to hear it, is remarkable.

This talent has made her a successful coach and consultant who helps women map out their life vision, reclaim their time, and transform their lives and work into exactly what they dreamed it would be.

In this book, Colene provides simple and actionable tools to help you shift your perspective and learn to flourish in your busy life.

With Colene's entertaining and casual writing style, these Monday Morning Pep Talks feel more like a chat with a wise best friend over a glass of sweet tea than excerpts from a book.

And by devoting just a few minutes a day to reading this book, you'll find yourself happier, more relaxed, more content, and truly thriving in your life...

...and you may even find yourself looking forward to Monday morning.

xoxo,
Molly

Molly Galbraith
Co-Founder and Woman-In-Charge
Girls Gone Strong

INTRODUCTION

Two and a half years ago, I started sending out a little weekly email I called Monday Morning Pep Talks. I (thankfully) had no idea at the time that these pep talks would turn into something like this. I wrote them for people, sometimes based on conversations we'd had the week before. I wrote them based off things I saw on social media. I wrote them for myself. A lot of weeks, these little messages were things that I personally very much needed to hear.

One of the things I loved about writing these, is that women would email and tell me I had read their mind. They would say things like, "get out of my journal" or "how'd you know I was going through this"?

Little did they know that mind reading is one -of

my party tricks!

HA! It's totally not, but I am good at reading people. I also know that if I'm going through something, someone else will be able to relate. We're never as alone as we think.

Every week, it's been my intention to give you something to inspire you. I wanted to give you something to focus on. I know what it's like to feel all over the place, and sometimes, focus can make all the difference. I wanted to give you something to show you that Mondays don't have to SUCK! In fact, they only feel like they suck because you've created some story about Monday… we all have.

Somewhere, along the way, society created this narrative that Mondays HAVE to be awful. That we should dread one day of the week, because it meant something. Poor Monday, it's done nothing to us, yet we walk around with all these hard feelings. We really need to have a conversation with Monday. Something along the lines of, "It's not you, it's me." Mondays are not the devil we've made it out to be.

My goal was to give Mondays some love. To give you something to look forward to on Mondays, and to inspire you to take action in your life, so you can achieve whatever you want. I wanted to share some stories. I wanted to give you tools. I wanted you to make a decision to create the life you wanted. I'm just along for the ride.

Why Mondays?

I was a cheerleader in middle school. I loved it. (Note: I once tried to convince my mom that I could be a professional cheerleader with the Dallas Cowboys!) Even though I would sometimes get confused on offense and defense, I loved that starting a cheer could shift the momentum of the crowd. I loved that we could show the players some support, and I loved the games where my team was the underdog, and we pulled off a major upset and win. I've always been one to root for the underdog, and that's how I feel about Mondays!

Statistic show that over 59% of Americans dread Monday Morning. In fact, the dread starts on Sunday nights. The Sunday Night Blues is a real thing. It starts around 6 p.m. with the realization that Monday is coming. And not in a "Game of Thrones'" Winter-is-coming kind of way... I mean in a real dread. Headaches, stomach aches and anxiety, are all symptoms of the Sunday Night Blues. Mondays are dreaded because it means a "back to reality", a shift in priorities, a daily grind that we've told ourselves needs to happen to be successful.

Let me be clear... I don't wake up every single Monday with the enthusiasm of a kid in a candy store. I have my days, just like everyone else. But, I've also learned how to not let one bad apple spoil the whole day!

To be honest, I don't always feel like writing these little pep talks. Sometimes, I think, no one will miss it if I don't send it out. But, I made this commitment to myself and to each and every person who has signed up over the years, that this would come out every single Monday.

And the short of it is, I was so freaking tired of starting things and not following through. So, I set a timer, and knock it out. Two years and some change later, here we are. The moral is: keep the promises you make to yourself and others. Your integrity will take you further than anything.

When I made the decision to write this book... timeout, I didn't really make the decision... I woke up at 3 a.m., and it seemed like God gave me the message to write this book. I know that sounds crazy, but it's true. So, here we are with this book. When I made the decision, I knew a few things:

• I don't want you to read it from cover to cover in one setting. Please, promise me you won't read it in a traditional way!

Nope!

What I really want is for you to flip it open to a random page and trust that it's giving you the exact message you need to hear. If the message doesn't resonate with you immediately, then think about how you could apply it.

• It's written for you. You may notice room for

you to put your name in. Sometimes it helps when you see your name to apply it to your life. Make it personal. It is personal... it's your life.

• It's not just for Mondays. Yes, this started with a Pep Talk for your Monday, but goodness, how many times have you hit a Thursday, and needed a bit of a pep? So, you can (and should) use this any day you need.

• Take Action. Once you read the Pep Talk, then take some action. If not, then you're totally wasting your time. You're not going to inspire your way to results, but you will totally take enough action to see results.

• Everything is better shared. Okay, not the flu, but everything else. Would you share this with a friend? Would you send this to someone who's in a bit of a rough patch? Would you share if something really moved you on Instagram? I'd love you forever if you did! Well, I'd totally love you forever anyway, but, I'd appreciate it!

These pep talks hit some major themes: love, success, spirituality, joy, leadership, changes, happiness, independence and forgiveness. In fact, those themes are weaved throughout the book a few times. Isn't that just like life? Sometimes we don't learn on the first shot.

What I really hope you take from this book is that intention can change your outcome. Being intentional with your day or your week can send

things into motion that create the life you want.

One of my readers said it best, I say what needs to be said in a firm and loving way. Think of me like your one best friend… you know the one that kinda has her act together, but is really more of a high-functioning hot mess. That's me in a nutshell.

The last thing I want to leave you with is this: I am not an extraordinary person. I'm not. I'm just a girl from small town Kentucky who's figured some things out and loves to share. Sometimes overshare. I'm someone who is still learning. Still growing. Still making mistakes. Still trying new things.

I'm still in this game of life with you, and instead of trying to figure it out alone, I think it could be much more fun to figure it out together!

1-2-3-4 let's go!

Love,
Colene

PS--- Want to get weekly inspiration? Get on the list: www.MondayMorningPepTalks.com.

YOU DESERVE IT

MONDAY MORNING PEP TALKS

YOU DESERVE IT!

Hey there _____!

<u>Your focus this week is on the things you deserve.</u>

Love, happiness, joy, health, peace of mind - these are things everyone deserves. These are not things you barter for or need to change yourself in order to earn them. Do you believe it?

Who you are today is deserving of a happy and peaceful life; the chaos is often found because you don't believe this.

When you don't believe you're worthy, you create situations and people that block your blessings. You allow people to treat you in ways that are not supporting your wellbeing. You treat yourself in ways that diminish your worth.

You think that if you just try harder or give more,

others will realize how much you've sacrificed, and be willing to give you what you need.

It just doesn't work that way. You must give yourself what you need first, and know that you are whole and enough just as you are... in all your imperfections and little quirks.

The best things in life you can't buy, so why would you try to bargain for them? They're FREE and they've always been yours, you just need to start claiming them!

This week, your challenge is to give yourself something that feels like love, happiness, joy, health or peace of mind. It can be a new workout. It can be a trip to the movies. It can be the new shirt you've been eyeing. Or a nap, just because it feels great. Whatever it is for you, make it a priority.

Have a great week!
xoxo-

Colene

DON'T BE THE ONLY THING STANDING IN YOUR WAY

MONDAY MORNING PEP TALKS

DON'T BE THE ONLY THING STANDING IN YOUR WAY

Hey _____!

<u>Your focus this week is to get out of your own way.</u>

Have you ever found yourself with an exciting idea or dream, but no clue how to achieve it?

I remember the first time I said I wanted to be the "next Oprah"... someone said it was cute, but what do you really want to do?

The "pipe dreams" go to the dreams graveyard and we give up on them. We end up reading books or watching movies about the people who went for it.

I watch a lot of those movies and read a lot of those books, and one thing that is consistent is they always say some variation of, "I got out of my own way and went for it."

Yes, the biggest thing in your way is YOU!

How do we do get in our own way?

By not trying, or giving up too soon.
We get overwhelmed by the goal, tell ourselves we're not good enough to achieve it, or write it off.
We try once, we get rejected and we never try again.

Do you know how many times JK Rowling got rejected for Harry Potter? 12... 12 NOs! 12 rejections. 12 times she could have given up.

What we fail to realize is that if we try, we may fail... in fact, we will more than likely fail the first time. But if we don't even try, we've already failed.

If we look at life as a holistic experience, we literally have nothing to lose, but so much to gain.

Lessons.
Experiences.
Perseverance.
Drive.

The next time you feel inspired to try something, make sure you're not in your own way. Allow yourself the chance to fail. Allow yourself the

chance to succeed. Don't stop before you even start.

Besides, when you're doing something you love, you're never failing, even if you do get a rejection letter!

What will you try this week?

Have a great week!

xoxo-

Colene

YOU
ARE
ENOUGH

MONDAY MORNING PEP TALKS

YOU ARE ENOUGH!

Hi friend---

Your focus this week is being enough.

Sometimes we need a reminder that we are enough just as we are. This week, I want you to remember that you are enough for anything that the week may throw at you.

You are enough:

Even when you feel ugly.
Even when you feel sad.
Even when the dress is a little too tight.
Even when you are doubtful.
Even when you feel jealous of others.
Even when you don't know what to do next.
Even when you feel overwhelmed.
Even when someone makes you feel small.
Even when you don't exercise.

Even when you eat the extra scoop of ice cream.
Even when you aren't the perfect parent.
Even when you wake up late.
Even when...

You are always enough!

<u>This week, keep track of all the things that make you amazing</u>.

Something you do well.
Something you're proud of.
Something you love about yourself.

And if you find yourself feeling guilty about something, remind yourself that you are enough, in spite of it.

Have a great week!

xoxo-

Colene

IT'S NOT THAT SERIOUS

MONDAY MORNING PEP TALKS

IT'S NOT THAT SERIOUS

Hi there---

<u>Your focus this week is on being less serious.</u>

When I was 16 I had the biggest crush on a guy name Jonathan. He was funny, smart, and just a nice guy. Every single time he would talk to me, it was a HUGE deal. Journal entries were written. Over-analyzing happened. I memorized every word, and every side look he'd give me.

When I go back and read the many many journal entries I wrote about dear ol' Jonathan all I can do is laugh! It's part romance novel, part supreme court brief weighing the pros and cons of a relationship that never actually happened.

Have you ever noticed how some things can seem

like such a big deal but then over time the feeling leaves.

What you thought mattered isn't that important. What you thought was really serious, isn't.

Time is our greatest teacher, and it's usually only with time can we see that it's maybe not THAT big of a deal.

Well that's exactly why you shouldn't take things so seriously!

Thoughts change. Feelings change. Ideas change.

You are meant to change and grow, and as you do, the importance of things will shift.

With that in mind, how bout we all be a little less serious about things, about life, about money , about work, about your body, about whatever you're going through.

Make sure it's worth it!

Your homework this week... RELAX, sister! Don't take yourself so seriously.

Have a great week!

xoxo-
Colene

YOU ARE
A
PRIORITY

MONDAY MORNING PEP TALKS

YOU ARE A PRIORITY

Hey there---

Your focus this week is on the front burner.

If you know me, you know I'm not much of a cook. It always seems overwhelming to me to know when to start things so everything's done close to the same time. It's a series of moving things from the front burner to the back burner. Rotating things in the oven. Prep and cleaning. Sometimes, I'll place something on the back burner and completely forget to check on it. Everything up front gets the attention. I've dried out rice, overcooked chicken, and made vegetables mush because I left them on the backburner too long.

What's something in your life that's on the proverbial backburner?

Most likely it's yourself , maybe your career.

Have you always loved art, but never make the time to create?

Do you love yoga, but don't make the time to go?

Maybe it's some other area that you're dying to pay some attention to.

Take some time this week to move something that's chillin, or drying out on the back burner back to the front, so you can pay it some attention.

Whatever it is you'd like to move front burner use the energy of this week to prioritize that.

Have a great week!

xoxo-

Colene

GIVE IT A LITTLE TIME

MONDAY MORNING PEP TALK

GIVE IT A LITTLE TIME

_____,

Your focus this week is on releasing the need to rush.

Are you in a hurry? Are you rushing from one thing to the next? Do you think if I could just hurry up and do _____ then I'll be happy?

Girl, stop rushing your life! Focus on where you're at and trust the process.

When you start rushing, it's a sign that you're not sure of the outcome... it's a sign of insecurity.

When we're unsure of the outcome, we then feel like we need to make it happen! When we force things we take away the beauty of feeling it happen.

I didn't get engaged until I was 33 years old. There were stages in my life that I wished it would have happened sooner. That I would have made it happen at 27 instead. But, y'all, no joke it happened at exactly the moment it was supposed to happen and not a second sooner… it's all about timing.

As I look back, I'm often okay with the pace of my life. I know that I wasn't ready for some of the things I use to dream about, and I'm happy to just take the time to learn and grow.

Notice **where you're trying to rush something along** in your life today.

Release the need to rush and **enjoy what's in front of you** with the security that it's going to happen anyway.

<u>Your homework for the week is to slow down and enjoy the pace of your life</u>. Ask yourself, what do I love most about this pace of life right now?

What's **for you** will never miss you! I promise!

Have a great week!

xoxo-

Colene

RELEASE TENSION. SET INTENTION.

MONDAY MORNING PEP TALKS

RELEASE TENSION. SET INTENTION.

Hi _____---

One of the most common things I hear when I ask clients about what's stopping them from achieving their goals is, "I just don't have the energy to do anything else."

I've learned a thing or two about energy. In fact, I recently got certified to be a Reiki practitioner (it's called attunement in the Reiki world), because I'm fascinated by energy in a human form.

Not to get too woo-woo on you this Monday, but we're all sources of energy. We're vibrating at different levels that attract or repel other sources of

energy.

So, I know that lack of energy is a common theme, especially for women, but did you know that energy is a renewable source for you. Hours are finite, energy isn't. You don't get energy, you generate it!

Let that sink in for a second... **You generate your energy.**

One of the things I would like you to think about this week is your energy leaks. Where are you giving your energy away? Where are you not even aware that you are leaking energy?

One huge source of energy leaks is lack of transitioning. We go from one thing to the next without releasing the energy from the previous thing. We end up carrying that energy into the next activity, and the next and the next... Do you know how much energy that's wasting?!?!?

I recently saw an interview with high-performance expert, Brendon Burchard... He gave this great mantra for transitions... **"Release tension. Set Intention".**

As you move from one thing to the next take one minute and slowly repeat the phrase, "release tension". Then take 30 seconds to set an intention for what you're about to do. Ask yourself, what do I want the outcome of this to be? or "How do I want to feel while I'm doing this?"

<u>So, this week, your challenge is to focus on better transitions.</u>

Don't just move from one thing to the next.

Transition.

Give yourself the gift of release and intention.

I would tell you the results for me (and some of my clients I've shared this with) but I'd rather hear them from you... Try it this week, and let me know how it works for you!

xoxo---

Colene

PULL A
TAYLOR

MONDAY MORNING PEP TALKS

PULL A TAYLOR

Hey Girl! Hey!

You may or may not know this about me, but I'm a HUGE Taylor Swift... now, before you go off and roll your eyes, let me explain. I heard Taylor's first song, "Tim Mcgraw", and thought it was such a sweet way to talk about a young romance. Then, shortly after, I saw Taylor perform at a Wal-Mart parking lot to a small crowd of people who were half-paying attention.

That was many years ago, but I remember thinking that she was having the best time ever, even though she wasn't playing a huge stadium. So, it's been crazy to see her skyrocket to stardom.

She recently released her new album, **Reputation**, and prior to the release, she cleared every bit of social media she had over the years. She came back as a "new" Taylor, who was re-inventing herself to who she wanted to be.

Her message, "like me or not, this is who I am."

Now, regardless of if you're #TeamTaylor or not, I think this is a valuable lesson for all of us.

If you don't like the story that's being told about you (even if it's to yourself), clear it out, and start again.

Change the narrative to who you want to be, and then become that person.

Just because you've never been the person who speaks up for herself doesn't mean you can't become that person.

Just because you've never been the person who works out three times a week, doesn't mean you can't become her.

Just because you've never been the person who's been "lucky" in love, doesn't mean you can't find true love... it's about changing the story!

You have the chance to wake up this morning and change the story you're telling yourself. Who do you want to be? If you were already her, what would she do today? How would she act? What

would she say?

This week, your focus is on pulling a Taylor, and re-invent yourself to whoever the h*ll you want to be!

xoxo---

Colene

KNOW YOUR WORTH

MONDAY MORNING PEP TALKS

KNOW YOUR WORTH

Hey there, _____,

Your focus this week is on **knowing your worth.**

Recently, an organization offered me $20,000 to come do some training for their employees. It would have been a great opportunity. It would have been a nice chunk of change. It would have been a step in a positive direction in building a long-term relationship with this organization. There were a lot of reasons to say "yes", but I said "no".

I turned it down.

Yes, I happily walked away from $20,000 and I don't regret it AT ALL!

I don't regret this decision because I (FINALLY) know my worth. The amount of training they were requesting, the number of hours, the strain on my voice and my body was worth WAY MORE than the amount they offered.

[Please allow me to toot my own horn... for just a sec.]

I'm a good trainer. Scratch that, I'm an excellent trainer. I get high marks for engagement, and I pride myself in not offering a "run of the mill" training. I have a gift to take semi-complex topics and make them relatable. This is a skill I've invested (money, development, etc.) in and developed over the course of the past 10-12 years.

So, toot toot, horn... TOOT TOOT!

This isn't me bragging, this is me owning a skill and a talent that I'm proud to have.

I said "no" because I didn't want to start questioning my own worth.

I said "no" because it didn't feel in alignment to who I am today, and the direction I'm going.

I said "no" because if I had said yes, I tell the world that I'm worth less than I know to be true.

Sometimes, you have to learn about the power of listening to your heart and forging your own path (and definition) of success. One that doesn't always line up with other people's expectations.

I've learned that true courage comes not only in what you say yes to but, more importantly, what you're willing to walk away from.

For me, true success is knowing, and appreciating my worth!

Know Your Worth

This week, I want you to start creating your ideas of your worth. I don't just mean money either. Sometimes figuring out your worth is as simple as recognizing you are worth respect in a heated conversation, or you are worth asking for additional help with the Holiday Dinner.

There are little ways we can show ourselves or ideas of our own worth. Those add up over time and before you know it, you're walking around with the confidence to say "no" to the things that devalue you!

I challenge you to come up with five "worth statements".

Here's how to start: I'm worth _____, because I _____.

Feel free to send me one or all that you come up with!

Have a great week!

xoxo-

Colene

THE

THINGS

YOU CAN

CONTROL

MONDAY MORNING PEP TALKS

THE THINGS YOU CAN CONTROL

_____,

Your focus this week is on **the things you can control.**

It's that time of year where everything seems a bit chaotic! Lot's of events, gift buying, expectations, etc. The hard part for most of us is the thought that we can control every aspect of our life. We have a plan, and dang-it, my life, holiday, gift plans, will go exactly how I have planned.

HA!

"If you want to make God laugh, tell him about your plans" - Woody Allen

The problem is often our plans are made with no room for slips or error. Our plans are made with perfect conditions. Then when one thing goes

wrong or the conditions are not perfect in reality, we can feel overwhelmed and frustrated.

Plans are great, but so is flow. Meaning, have a plan but also be open to the natural flow of the situation.

It Snows In Flagstaff

On my recent trip out west, we drove from Las Vegas to Sedona AZ. As we were driving, we saw a sign that said "WARNING! WINTER WEATHER REPORTED AHEAD!"

Wait, what? It's not supposed to snow, we're out west... but it did! I don't mean a little snow, I mean a big snow storm that covered the roads and highway. It was dark. There were accidents around us, and (thankfully) my guy was driving.

It would have been super easy to be frustrated, but I have absolutely no control over the weather. I couldn't change the conditions, but I could focus on the one thing I could control... my attitude!

The whole rest of the drive I started giving my guy pep talks and telling him how thankful I was for his driving skills. I focused on encouraging him instead of complaining about the stupid snowstorm (I can call it that now, right?)

What can you control?

This week, I want you to focus on what you can control: attitude, perspective, creativity, response, etc.

Everything else, YOU CAN'T CONTROL! So, let it go!

There will be a family member who doesn't know how to act. There will be delays. There will be traffic (especially at the mall). There will be a failed baking attempt. There will be many things out of your control, but this week focus on all the things you can.

When we focus on what we can control, we give ourselves the power to change (not always the outcome) but how we view the outcome. We don't waste our precious energy on things out of our control! Do you know how big of a gift that is to yourself?

Tis the season for gifts, right?

Have a great week!

xoxo-

Colene

THE ATTITUDE OF GRATITUDE

MONDAY MORNING PEP TALKS

THE ATTITUDE OF GRATITUDE

Hey friend,

Your focus this week is on **gratitude.**

I can't believe we're already in November. During the month of Thanksgiving, it's only appropriate that we focus on gratitude.

I've been a big believer of focusing on gratitude as a means of changing my energy. Meaning, if I'm feeling run-down, or upset, or frustrated, I force myself to quickly list three things I'm thankful for in that moment. It's really hard to be angry and grateful at the same time, so I shift my attention to gratitude.

What would your day look like if you focus on gratitude?

Gratitude as a practice.

This week, spend 5 minutes a day writing down three things you're thankful for in your life. Then, take it one step further and list three reasons why you're thankful.

This is a practice that will transform how you look at your life and the world! Try it on for size, and let me know how it goes.

Have a great week!

xoxo-

Colene

BECAUSE I WANT TO

MONDAY MORNING PEP TALKS

BECAUSE I WANT TO

———————,

I remember when I was growing up, I would ask my mom to buy me a piece of candy, a fun outfit, or a Nintendo game, and inevitably, she would ask me "why I needed it."

I very rarely needed it... but I always wanted it.

In my mind, that should have been enough.

Now, I know there is a lot of good from not giving kids everything they want. I know we should learn to appreciate the things we have. I also know that women are taught to put everyone (their needs, wants, desires, etc.) ahead of themselves. We are taught that our own wants come last, and that we should be able to justify our reasons... I call BS!

I've spent the last few years learning the value in my own wants... their worth, and my happiness.

Here's the thing, we spend way too much of our lives denying ourselves things we want because we think it's "too much", or "not necessary", or our parents/spouses/ significant other's aren't on the same page, or whatever reason we tell ourselves.

Sometimes, the person we need to convince the most is looking at us in the mirror.

This week, your task is to do, get, have something just because you want it!

No guilt.

No sorrys.

Nothing but pure joy because you chose yourself!

Your wants have value.
Your desires have value.
You deserve to put yourself on the front-burner.

So, sleep in on Sunday. Take the yoga class you've wanted to take because it makes you feel better. Buy the purse. Eat out. Say no. Say yes.

Whatever you want to do (within reason of course), do it!

Have a great week!

Colene

Colene H. Elridge

FORGIVENESS CAN YOU IMAGINE?

MONDAY MORNING PEP TALKS

FORGIVENESS. CAN YOU IMAGINE?

Last week was the anniversary of my father's death. Though it's been a long time since his death, the day still comes in with a bit of a sting.

My father committed suicide.

It's not something I talk about often, though it's something that's shaped much of my life. It took me years to find a path for forgiveness. Four years ago I made a decision to forgive him. Not just for his choice, but for the life I thought I would have if he were still here. I've written about this before in my column on KY Forward, so some of you may be familiar with my story.

I'm not exaggerating one bit when I tell you it is hands down the very best thing I've ever done.

Every year, I now make a commitment to keep forgiving my father. I forgive him all over again as a way to remind myself that my love for him is much stronger than the anger, regret, or pain that still from time to time rises up within me.

Forgiveness is a powerful tool. Forgiveness allowed me to stop holding on to something that wasn't mine to hold. Forgiveness is strength and gave me the strength to start living more in my purpose.

Here's one of my favorite quotes on forgiveness:

"Forgiveness does not relieve someone of responsibility for what they have done. Forgiveness does not erase accountability. It is not about turning a blind eye or even turning the other cheek. It is not about letting someone off the hook or saying it is okay to do something monstrous. Forgiveness is simply about understanding that every one of us is both inherently good and inherently flawed. Within every hopeless situation and every seemingly hopeless person lies the possibility of transformation."

- Desmond Tutu, The Book of Forgiving: The Fourfold Path for Healing Ourselves and Our World

This week, your task is to FORGIVE someone in your life. Forgive them for yourself and for your future. No need to have a big elaborate forgiveness ceremony (unless you want to). No need to even let the person know that they are forgiven. Do this to give yourself the peace you deserve.

Forgiveness is peace.
Forgiveness is strength.
Forgiveness is love.

Have a great week!

Colene

YOU'RE AMAZING. JUST THE WAY YOU ARE.

MONDAY MORNING PEP TALKS

YOU'RE AMAZING. JUST THE WAY YOU ARE.

Do you ever feel like you can't be 100% yourself? At work? At home? At social events? Do you ever feel like if you were your authentic self, no one would like you, hire you, or want to be your friend?

I get it.

If you've ever felt the need to "shrink", play small, or be "less" than your wonderful, amazing self, this week's Pep Talk is for you.

Enter my sorority sister, Drew.

Drew is an incredible woman. She's unapologetically opinionated. She's brilliant (she's not gonna play dumb to stroke your ego). She not quiet. By that I mean she's loud... not in a bad way, but I'd imagine she's louder than your average gal.

We bonded over both being called "bossy girls" when we were young. She's full of energy. She's a cross-fitter. She LOVES to wear a shiny crown and pink boa on her birthday.

Oh, and she's an attorney!

A couple of years ago, she and her husband moved to Texas where she worked for a very prestigious law firm. Although she was a rockstar at her job, she said she didn't feel like she was valued or appreciated for the work she was doing or her approach.

So, she left. She went to a new firm, and rolled in like the storm that she is. Drew was told she was hired for her approach, personality, and the perspective she was bringing to the firm.

So Drew, kept on being Drew.

364 days later... yes, one day shy of a year... my sweet and amazing friend was offered PARTNER at her firm. She was recognized and rewarded for being completely herself!

I asked her to tell me how being given the chance to be authentically Drew changed how she approached work, and here's what she had to say:
The freedom to be my authentic self at work — and be respected for that authentic self — is absolutely life-changing and powerfully affirming. As Coach Colene could tell you, loud, opinionated, intense, and Type-A are all apt words one could use to describe me. But the

*words loyal, silly, sarcastic, and maybe even funny
should be in the mix as well.*

*One of the reasons I made the switch to a new firm was a
promise from the CEO that we'd have fun if I came to
work there. Having never heard a lawyer place a value
on fun, I almost fell out of my chair. Not only has the
CEO kept that promise, but my immediate boss did as
well. It's that boss (who insists he's not my boss) that
really has made all the difference.*

*Once, a partner jokingly told me that my boss had
"empowered me." Without missing a beat, my boss
responded "Like I need to do anything to empower the
force of nature that is Drew." He has been a never
ending cheerleader and is 100% committed to building
me up, making me successful and being an advocate for
my continued advancement within the organization.
And as I'm sure everyone reading this knows, having
an advocate is the most critical piece of one's success in
an organization.*

*Like many high-achieving women I know, I struggle
daily with an ever-present impostor syndrome. But the
level of support I have received at my new firm has
allowed me to focus on being the best lawyer I can and
not be encumbered by the ever present nagging question
of "Do these people think I'm good enough?" On the
contrary – they've always communicated to me that not
only am I good enough, I actually am a rock star. There's
absolutely nothing more rewarding than someone
communicating "I believe in you – ALL of you."*

Here's what I love about Drew's story, it's a
reminder to know your values, know your worth,

and be yourself. **<u>Success will totally find you.</u>** Someone will appreciate you and all you bring to the table. It's also a great reminder about the importance of an advocate (especially at work)... but that's a Pep Talk for another time.

<u>This week, your task is to find the area(s) of your life where you're not being 100% authentically yourself.</u> What are you scared will happen if someone sees the real you? How can you start to dial-up your authentic self? Pick one are and show the world who you really are!

Gurl, we need you to be yourself! As Drew's boss told her, "I believe in you - ALL of you."

Have a great week!

xoxo-

Colene

PS - Y'all are such incredible women. I'm so thankful for each and every one of you!

YOU CAN GO AND LOVE YOURSELF

MONDAY MORNING PEP TALKS

YOU CAN GO AND LOVE YOURSELF.

Happy Love Week!

I love this week, because I think it's such a reminder that there are all kinds of love!

Regardless of the external love that you may (or may not) have in your life, it all starts with the love you have for yourself.

Here are some ways that you can "love yourself":

1. Surround yourself with people who love and encourage you.

2. Start with a bang. Every morning, tell yourself something positive. If it makes you smile, say it!

3. Be mindful of what you think, feel and want. Start living your life in ways that reflect that.
4. You are what you eat. Eat the foods that make you feel great. Not just in the moment, but in the

future. Don't get me wrong, I love ice cream, and my gummy bears, but I know I can't live off of them.

5. Treat other with love and respect. How you treat others is a reflection on how you feel about yourself. Give yourself some love... Actually, give yourself a lot of love!

6. Learn to say no. It's a complete sentence. No need to explain, or try to talk around it!

7. Forgive yourself. That thing you did (or didn't do) one time that still makes you feel embarrassed, bad, shame... It's time to let that go! Learn from it, and move on.

8. Find your happy. Is it walking in the woods, drinking a cup of tea, or reading a good book? Whatever it may be... do more of it. Schedule it!

9. Gratitude. Find something to be thankful for every day. WRITE IT DOWN! Like, for real... the more you recognize the things you have to be thankful for, the more you'll have!

10. Have fun! Get out there and do the things that light you up! Enjoy them!

This week, your task is to find ways to practice more self-love. You can cultivate the love you want from others by creating it for yourself. It's the little things that add up to great love!

Just in case no one tells you this week... I totally love you! Like, for real love you, and so incredibly thankful that you give me a little space in your life! (((HUGS)))

Have a great week!

xoxo-

Colene

GIRLS JUST WANNA HAVE FUN

MONDAY MORNING PEP TALKS

GIRLS JUST WANNA HAVE FUN

Hey _____!

Your focus this week is on **<u>Having Fun.</u>**

I want to tell you a little secret... Life is supposed to be fun! It really is!

I can't imagine that God, the Universe, or whatever you may or may not believe in created us to walk around our entire lives unhappy, bored and unenthused. We often make choices that lead us to feeling unhappy, and struggle to shift back into joy.

When was the last time you had fun? I mean real unapologetic fun!

Was it that long ago?

Fun is not a bad word. Even if you're a mom, or wife, or daughter, or business owner, or aunt, or

worker, or whatever title you may have. You are still allowed to have fun in your life.

So, **this week, have FUN.**

Do something that seems fun to you (even if everyone else thinks it's weird). Bonus points if you bring a friend along with you!

What kind of fun are you getting into this week?

Have a fun week!

xoxo-

Colene

PS - Fun is one of my core values! Excited for you to have fun this week!

HELLO, I'M TRYING TO FOCUS

MONDAY MORNING PEP TALKS

HELLO, I'M TRYING TO FOCUS

Your focus this week is on **just one thing.**

Raise your hand if you have too many balls in the air... I'll wait!

Still waiting for you to put one of your obligations down, so you can raise your hand...

Sometimes, we spread our focus to several things (some which may not be as important as we think).

What happens when you focus on too many things? What happens when you have too many balls in the air? What happens when you spread yourself way too thin?

What happens...

You get frustrated. Your fuse is shorter. You take yourself for granted. You judge yourself (and others). You don't do your best work. The balls come crashing down. Then you get frustrated again. It's cyclical.

We both know that when you have too much going on, you're not at your best self, and if you're not at your best, **you can't give your best**.

This week I want you to focus on one thing, and just one thing. You pick. Give it all your energy, and see what happens. Now, this is not to say that you won't have to do other things in the week, we all have obligations, but I want to challenge you to be mindful of the energy you give to the things that are not important.

Focus my dear, focus!

Enjoy your week!

xoxo-

Colene

CAN YOU DO IT? YES, YOU CAN.

MONDAY MORNING PEP TALKS

CAN YOU DO IT? YES, I CAN!

Your focus this week is on **hyping yourself up!**

This may surprise some of y'all, but I still get really nervous before I teach a workshop, give a talk, or appear on tv. I'll spare you every detail, but I get sweaty, my heart starts racing, and I know my voice goes a couple of octaves higher.

I literally competed in public speaking from 6th grade through college on local, state, and national levels. I was once awarded a spot in the top 10% of collegiate speakers in the nation… yet, I still feel a high sense of nerves before every speech.

Now, for me, this is an annoyance, but not something that stops me from going out there to inspire people. For others, their fear stops them in their tracks.

I wanted to share this little trick I learned on how to hype myself up before I do something that I might feel a little anxious about.

Instead of just telling myself, "Colene, you can do this!' or "Colene, you're awesome." I'll ask myself a simple question, "Can you do this? And if so, how?"

Here's the thing, **I love telling myself I'm awesome**. I also, love hearing myself talk, but if I ask myself, Colene, can you do this, and if so, how... I have to respond. I have to answer, which forces me to think, to plan, and to muster up my motivation. It becomes an **active process instead of a passive one**.

No need to over think this, just think of 2-3 ways that you know you're ready.

Your assignment this week is to choose an active form of hyping yourself up. It's as simple as, Colene, can you do this? If so, how?

Enjoy your week!

xoxo-

Colene

PS- You're amazing! Just thought I'd remind you! :)

WE CAN BE HEROES

MONDAY MORNING PEP TALKS

WE CAN BE HEROES

It's Memorial Day, and I'm always overwhelmed with the gratitude for the men and women who have died serving our country. I have a lot of military connections in my life and I'm often inspired by their bravery and courage. They are truly heroes in my eyes.

When I think what it means to be a hero, I think of someone who shows courage in the face of fear, someone who takes a risk, and someone who is resilient in the face of challenges.

Do you have to go to war to be a hero? Of course not! So how can you start being a hero in your own life?

Years ago, I was frustrated with my job, my boss, the direction of my career... basically, **all the thing**! I remember having a conversation with my brother, complaining about everything that was

wrong in my life, and he looked me dead in the eyes and said, "Colene, no one's just going to offer you a job... what are you doing to get a new job?"

Now, it was a shock to my system, because I think I was truly waiting around for some random company to call me (out of the blue) and offer me a job. That was never going to happen. That hard-truth from my brother changed how I thought about a lot of things...

No one is coming to rescue you.
Not your mama.
Not Oprah.
Not the government.
Nothing is en route to save you.
Not your new diet.
Not your accolades.
Not winning the blame game.
No safety net is solid.
Not the corner office.
Not downward facing dog.
Not the white picket fence or "happily ever after" or having six figures in your bank account.
You are the missing link of your liberation.
Pick the lock.
Turn the key.
Burn the ties that bind.
It's time to set yourself free.

-L'Erin Alta

Your focus this week is on **being your own hero!**

Stop waiting for someone else to solve your problems, and step boldly towards your truth. Stop pondering and start doing. Stop complaining and start changing. We owe it to ourselves, and to those who gave their all to live a life worth living!

Happy Memorial Day!

Enjoy your week,

xoxo-

PICTURE IT

MONDAY MORNING PEP TALKS

PICTURE IT...

Your focus this week is on **seeing your vision for your best life.**

I spent most of my Sunday watching reruns of the Golden Girls.

Gosh, I love that show!

It's a show that features strong female friendships, and how important that is in our lives.

One of my favorite parts of the show is when Sophia says, "Picture it, Sicily, 1937..." She then goes into some crazy story with such detail, it's like you get transformed back in time.

The power of visualization allows you to see what you want for your life BEFORE you actually have it. I spend a good bit of time visualizing my

success, and how I want my life to look. Kinda like daydreaming, but with a bit more purpose.

Do you remember when you were young and you could play pretend? You were whatever your mind believed you to be... a princess, the president, or even Oprah (in my case). The world was as big as you could imagine, and you could be anything you wanted to be.

This week, I want you to spend 10 minutes visualizing your best self... what do you look like? What are you doing? How are you feeling, and why? What are you wearing? What's your career? Set a timer, close your eyes, and start to pretend you are already there.

When you can see it, then you can be it!

Dream big, my dear!

Enjoy your week,

xoxo-

Colene

JUST
DANCE

MONDAY MORNING PEP TALKS

JUST DANCE

Hey there---

Over the weekend I went to a pretty amazing dance program designed to allow children with special needs to perform. It was beautiful! It was touching! Mostly, it was inspiring to see how these children lit up on the stage.

Right before the show started, one of the performers was talking with her family, and when someone said, "Don't get nervous," she looked them dead in their eyes and said, "pfffff... I don't get nervous. I got this."

I wanted to go over there and high-five her for her confidence. When I tell you all she nailed her dance, she completely got every move and danced like she was performing for the American Ballet

Theater. She was amazing, and in no way let her disability deter her from her greatness.

Your focus this week is on finding confidence in big and small ways.

What area of your life do you have confidence, but you're still playing small? Do you make the best brownies? Are you a killer negotiator? Do you rock the mom game hard? Are you a leader in your field?

Where can you express your confidence just a tad bit more? Or better yet, where can you stop diminishing your strengths? You do things like say, "Oh, that's no big deal" or "I'm just a [insert super cool thing here]".

One of my favorite quotes is by Marianne Williamson, "...Your playing small does not serve the world".

The young dancer this weekend showed how much confidence can change the entire game for you. Play a bigger game. Own your strengths. Dance like you're a dag gone Rockette!

Boogie On-

Colene

TRY
A
LITTLE

MONDAY MORNING PEP TALKS

TRY A LITTLE

This week your challenge is to **<u>try something new.</u>**

Let's be honest, it can be terrifying to try new things. We get caught up in life and responsibilities, and it's hard to branch out of our comfort zone. But we don't start out like this.

I spent my entire childhood in a one of two camps:
1. I don't want to do anything… Brownies, Girl Scouts, sports, or any variety of activities that my mom "encouraged" me to try.
2. I'll do EVERYTHING. My high school and college time was spent making up for loss time. I did it all!

The problem, was I was a by-the-book overachiever. It went from me just trying something out to being president of the organization. If I was going to be a part of something, I was going to lead it! (hello burnout!)

Then all of a sudden, we graduate into the "real world" and are expected to know exactly what we're good at, what we like to do, and how we like to spend our time. New activities or experiences grind to a halt, and it's almost expected that we will "settle into" nothing more than work and home. Months and years pass by, and we haven't so much as tried a new drink, because we're comfortable with what we know.

The truth is, we very rarely try new things because we don't have to.

Even though no one is forcing us to try something new. And even though we don't have to, we should.

<u>Trying new things teaches you</u> so much about yourself. You can see where you default to an excuse or when you're willing to push through. There's a lot of power in being a beginner. You learn how to extend some grace for yourself. You learn how to take more control over the things you want in your life. It teaches you how to find adventure in both big and small things.

If you've ever thought, "That would be fun to try!" or "I wish I could… [take ballet lessons, paint, learn

a language, travel to a new country, start a blog, learn how to code, etc...], then I urge you to listen to your inner adventurer and try! What's the worst that can happen?

What do you want to try this week?

xoxo---

Colene

PS--- Take a picture of you trying something new and tag Coach Colene in it! :)

GET THE PEBBLE OUT OF YOUR SHOE

MONDAY MORNING PEP TALKS

GET THE PEBBLE OUT OF YOUR SHOE

Hiya!

This week your challenge is to **get the pebble out of your shoe.**

Muhammad Ali said, "It isn't the mountains ahead to climb that wear you out, it's the pebble in your shoe." Can you imagine walking all day, every day with a small pebble in your shoe? The pebble would constantly rub your skin, and aggravate the heck out of you...

The truth, most of us are walking around with a pebble in our shoes every single day. And if I'm really honest, we usually have several pebbles rolling around in our shoes. The pebbles are the little things that we just tolerate every day. Maybe

it's the remote that needs new batteries, maybe it's organizing your closet so it doesn't take you so long to find something to wear to work. Maybe it's going through the pile of junk mail sitting on your kitchen table (note these are all real for me). Or, maybe there are emotional pebbles you need to tackle. Emotional pebbles like stress, anxiety, and frustration.

Whatever your pebbles are, this week I want you to start to remove them. One by one.

You see these pebbles are draining you. These pebbles are rubbing you raw. These pebbles are weighing you down.

When you start removing them, you free yourself and your energy to focus on bigger and better things... the mountain (aka your life).

So, get those pebbles out your dang shoes!

xoxo---
Colene

GET WHAT
YOU WANT

MONDAY MORNING PEP TALKS

GET WHAT YOU WANT

This week your challenge is to **get what you want.**

A few days ago I was walking around Target, and a little girl (about 4 or 5) was in complete meltdown mode.

There was screaming.

There was crying.

There was a full layout in the middle of the floor.

As I walked by, I mouthed to her mother, "It's alright."

A few minutes later (as I tend to meander around Target), I saw the same little girl laughing, and eating some candy. Girlfriend got exactly what she wanted, and was now having the best time.

Now, I'm not judging anyone's parenting, cause totally not my place. But, I'm gonna go on and call this girl my hero of the day!

You see, so many times we give up quickly on the things we want. We're not willing to throw a fit about it, cause we don't want to seem too aggressive. And we settle for something that's a fraction of what we deserve.

I'm not saying we all throw fits, but what if we demanded just a little bit more for ourselves...

What if you don't take the first salary offer cause you know you're worth more?

What if, you send your food back because it wasn't what you actually ordered?

What if you call someone out for trying to mansplain something to you?

What if you say "no" to being on the committee that you really don't have time for?

What if you just said, "Thank you" to a compliment, instead of trying to talk the person out of the compliment... you know, "Oh, this dress, I got it on sale, it's no big deal."

What if you allowed yourself to get exactly what you want, simply because you want it? How amazing would that be?

This week, I want you to find one area in your life
to get exactly what you want. Feel free to start
small. Then work your way up to the bigger things.

xoxo---

Colene

PS--- Not to sound too cheesy, but you're worth it!

Colene H. Elridge

WHO ARE YOU MEANT TO BE?

MONDAY MORNING PEP TALKS

WHO ARE YOU MEANT TO BE?

Hi friend,

This week your challenge is to **focus on who you're meant to be.**

How many times have you stood in your own way? How many times have you stopped yourself from doing something because you got scared? How many times have you stopped just before you reached your goal because it was becoming too real?

Why do you stop yourself from reaching your full potential?

I know it's super scary to think about who you could be at your absolute best... Then there are expectations, right? Then there are the people asking, "Well, who do they think they are"? Then there is the fear of failure.

I get it!

But I also get that it's exhausting to keep living as a fraction of who you are meant to be.

Who are you meant to be?

Brilliant!

Extraordinary!

Perfectly Imperfect!

A few months ago, I woke up at 3:30 am and wrote the following:

On judgment day, God will not ask, "Why were you not the next Oprah?" Instead, God will ask, "Why were you not Colene?" The goal in life is not to attain some imaginary ideal or be a watered down version of someone else; the goal is to find and fully use your own gifts... in your own way.

It was my own personal wake-up call to play a bigger game! It's lonely to play a bigger game by yourself, so I want to invite you to do the same.

You already have it inside of you...

You just need to **get out of your own dang way!**

xoxo---

Colene

FIND
THE
JOY

MONDAY MORNING PEP TALKS

FIND THE JOY

Hi there _____-

The last couple of weeks have been heavy… I mean waking up in the middle of the night feeling overwhelmed by the world's events. It's in those moments that I remember I am not meant to solve ALL the world's problems. I can't… and when I think it's all on my shoulders, that's when I feel fear, doubt, and lack.

This week, with everything going on, <u>I want you to focus on joy!</u>

I'm not suggesting you bury your head in the sand. I'm not suggesting you don't speak out for what is wrong. What I am suggesting is to not let it weigh you down every second of every day.

So find joy in your everyday life.

Find joy in your morning drive.
Find joy in your family.
Find joy in your workout.
Find joy in your sleep. (Yes, please!)
Find joy in your food.
Find joy in your bad tv choices.
Find joy in your work.
Find joy in your outfit.
Find joy in your phone calls.
Find joy in yourself…

Just find joy wherever you can this week. Make it your top priority!

I find that I can't speak up, or fight racism, or even coach women into strong leaders if I'm not filling my cup with joy.

So, you want to do your best work?

<u>Find joy in your life</u> and then do the work!

Have a great week!

With Joy----
   Colene

I'M
BAD

MONDAY MORNING PEP TALKS

I'M BAD

Hey girl! Hey!

This week your challenge is to **be bad at something.**

So, if you follow me on Instagram, you may have seen I took my very first dance class over the weekend. In my mind I dance like Beyonce' , but in reality... let's just say not so much.

It was funny for me to watch myself in the mirror be BAD! I mean really bad at something. It was also really humbling to be a beginner.

I was the oldest in the class by at least 10 years, and the 11-year-old dancer in the class was so amazing that I found myself trying to follow her as they were teaching the moves.

Did I mention that it was a lyrical contemporary class? One that requires you to move with grace and ease from one move to the next... not really my strength.

But, I'm gonna go back!

You see there's so much you learn about yourself when you're bad at something. It would have been easy for me to leave or decide to sit out and observe. When you put yourself out there, it requires you to realize there are so many things you don't know, and so many things you can learn.

We don't give ourselves time to be a beginner at anything past a certain age. Be in the energy of learning, where everything is fun, and exciting, and terrifying, and all the things wrapped into one.

<u>So this week, your focus is on letting yourself be bad at something new.</u> Maybe take an online language class. Maybe it's gardening to improve your green thumb. Or, maybe it's taking a dance class for the first time. Whatever it is, just be okay with not being an instant professional. Be a beginner, and be excited about learning!

Have a great week!

xoxo---

Colene

PS--- When the instructor asked me what my goals were for the class, I said, "I just want to have fun. I mean I'm not trying to audition for Juilliard or anything." She was shocked that anyone wanted to do something just to do it.

SUCCESS IS NOT A BURDEN

MONDAY MORNING PEP TALKS

SUCCESS IS NOT A BURDEN

Your focus this week is all on your success...

I, like so many of you, have fears. I remember talking with someone about how scared I was, not of failure, but of success. I was worried about what that meant for me, for my family, for my friendships, and my life.

What would it mean if I was too successful?

What would people think about me?

Would people think I got too big for my britches (as my mom would say)?

I felt that the more success I had the smaller I wanted to become. It was scary. It felt like a burden to everyone around me. I worried if I asked for anything, people would think I was a diva!

I'm not sure if you've ever felt this way, but here's what I've learned.

Your success is not a burden. Your needs, wants, and desires are valid. In fact, your success only adds to the lives of those around you.

It's possible that someone may have told you that if you asked for something you needed or wanted that you were selfish. It's possible that you believed it, and continued to silence your needs. You then got in the habit of never speaking up. Never asking. Always trying to do it alone.

Today, make yourself the promise to end it now!

Your needs. Your Wants. Your goals matter.

I want you to know that you can be successful AND loving. You can ask for what you need AND help someone else. You can receive a compliment AND be a good person.

Learn to trust your gut, and know that everything you want, need, desire is not a burden... you are not a burden!

You, my friend, are a gift to the world!

xoxo---

Colene

OPEN

+

CONNECT

MONDAY MORNING PEP TALKS

OPEN + CONNECT

Sunday night I ran into yoga class with two
minutes left to spare.

I'm glad I made it.
I'm glad I looked in my backseat and saw spare
yoga clothes.
I'm glad I listened to the voice that said: "Go".

During class, the instructor said, "I want you to
focus on being open and connecting to your body,
and know that you are supported".

As we moved into postures, I realized how much
my body (and mind) needed moments of
intentional movement. This particular class moves

very slowly through postures, in fact, you hold most postures for 2-7 minutes.

It's challenging because it forces you to feel (I mean really feel) your body.

But then, there's this moment that you think, "I don't really want to hold this posture any longer." Then you hold it and you feel this release.

It's amazing!
It's freeing.
It's what you didn't know you needed.

So this week, I want to challenge you to focus on how you can feel more open and connected to yourself. How can you sit two beats longer with something that may be uncomfortable to get to the release? How can you listen to your body and intuition more, and trust the truth of what you hear?

This can apply to so many areas of your life. Pick one, sit with it, move with it, hold it, and feel the release!

xoxo---

Colene

DON'T START YOUR WEEK WITHOUT THIS...

MONDAY MORNING PEP TALKS

DON'T START YOUR WEEK WITHOUT THIS...

The time between Thanksgiving and Christmas is always such a weird time for me. It's a time where the "best of" list (movies, music, most fascinating people, etc.) come out, and a time where everyone seems to be reflecting on the year that's been.

There are moments that it seems 2017 just started and times when it seems it's taken 2 years time. That's the thing with time, it's all relative. We overestimate what we can do in a day (I've seen your to-do list) and underestimate what we can do in a lifetime!

This is a time where it's easy to want to sit and let the rest of the year float by... don't! There's still time left to do the things you said you wanted to do.

How?

I'm so glad you asked... Get out pen and paper, and ask yourself these three questions:

1. How do I want to FEEL for the rest of the year? Go on and set the intention.

2. What thoughts do I need to THINK to create those feelings? It all starts with your thoughts... your mind is a powerful tool.

3.What can I do today that lets me FEEL the feelings I desire? I mean, what are the actions you can do?

You can do this DAILY, right after you wake up. Give yourself the chance to create the day you want instead of the day running you.

I can't wait to see how you finish 2017 strong!

xoxo---

Colene

YOU DON'T HAVE TO BE AVAILABLE

MONDAY MORNING PEP TALKS

YOU DON'T HAVE TO BE AVAILABLE

One of my favorite quotes is, "You don't have to attend every argument you're invited to."

I love it, because it's such a powerful reminder that you have a choice, and just because you are invited, you can decline. It got me thinking about other things you don't have to be available for.

You don't have to be available:
- to the committee
- to old habits
- to the party invitation
- to the bake sale at your kid's school
- to do something the way your parents did it
- to hold on to something that's not serving you
- to stay at a job just because it's comfortable

- to remain silent because it's easy
- to speak up about everything
- to burnout
- to making more than one meal for your family per night
- to doing things the hard way
- to life being hard
- to the beliefs that you had last year, yesterday, or a second ago
- BS
- to frustration

You see, you don't have to be available to anything you don't want to give your energy to,

Your challenge this week is to make a list of the things you are no longer available for this year.

Start it like this:

I [insert name here], am no longer available for:

Then go to town!

You deserve your best energy. You deserve to have your wants and desires. You deserve all the best this life has to offer... stop settling for anything less!

xoxo---

Colene

PS--- Feel free to share with me!

YOU ARE WORTH MORE

MONDAY MORNING PEP TALKS

YOU ARE WORTH MORE

Your focus this week is on **You Are Worth More.**

When I first started my business I did A LOT of speaking engagements for free. I knew it was part of growing my brand, getting my name out, and building reputability. It was hard because I would invest tons of time and energy into creating a great presentation. I wanted them to see the value in what I did. I wanted to show them they got a whole lot of BANG for their buck. Then, I wanted them to hire me!

The problem is it became exhausting. People started expecting me to do everything for free. I was burnt out!

How can I give value without running myself ragged?
How can I continue to serve and pay my bills?

It was an ongoing struggle for me.

The biggest struggle was feeling like I wasn't valuable, even if I knew (at least on a surface level) that I was.

One day, an organization asked me to put together a proposal to do several days of speaking at their event. I was excited. I put together a dynamic line-up of topics, and workshops, and activities. I submitted the proposal, and the organizer emailed back and said, "Oh, we were hoping you'd do it for free for the exposure."

Now, I can share with you the numbers on the amount women get paid to speak versus men. I can show you how for women of color that number is even more concerning. But, the piece that is most alarming is this conference had big sponsors, a high ticket cost, and expected several hundred individuals in attendance. But they wanted several days of my time for free...

I was angry!
I was beyond frustrated.
I felt a sense of worthlessness... How could they not see the value?

I sat down to write in my journal. Journaling is the best way for me to get everything out of my head, and give it the space it needs for clarity. Journaling also gives me answers... I jokingly call them my "divine downloads" because so many times I'll read the words that are on the page and wonder where they came from.

That day, I wrote the following: **"Don't confuse what you're offered for what you're worth."**

That was a big wake-up call for me. It made me become more aware of my time, my energy, and my thoughts.

Listen, you may ask for the raise, and they said no. You may ask for the sale, and get rejected. You may not get what you asked for... or you may get exactly what you asked for.

Your worth is not contingent on any of that. Your worth is only as valuable as you believe yourself to be!

What I know though, is you are worth more than you probably think.

This week, I want you to focus on discovering your worth. How are you owning all the talents and gifts you have to offer?

xoxo---
Colene

PS--- Can I give you a challenge? If you're planning to attend any type of professional development this year, look for diversity with the presenters. If there isn't any, maybe ask the organizers to look into more diverse presenters. You can learn so much from different perspectives!

CHOOSE YOUR THOUGHTS

MONDAY MORNING PEP TALKS

CHOOSE YOUR THOUGHTS

Your focus this week is on **<u>Choosing Your
Thoughts.</u>**

The quickest way to make a change is to change
your thoughts about it. I know that sounds both
simple and hard. But the truth is, you can't control
circumstances, but you can have some control over
your thoughts. Our thoughts trigger everything
else, our feelings, actions, results... so if we can
manage to change the thought, we can make the
change a bit easier.

Here's a simple way to do this...

Today I choose:
Peace over Perfection.
Heart over Hustle.
Calm over Chaos.
Faith over Fear.

Flow over Frustration.
Alignment above all else.

You see when you make the choice to be in alignment with who you want to be, how you want to feel, and what you want to do... it changes everything!

Your challenge this week: Within the first five minutes of waking up, ask yourself the following question: "How do I want to feel today?" One word!

Name it!
Claim it!
Become it!

Do this every day this week, and give yourself reminders throughout the day.

Here's to choosing good thoughts!

xoxo---

Colene

PS--- I'd LOVE for you to share your word on social media and tag me in it! Can't wait to see your week unfold!

IS IT
IMPORTANT?

MONDAY MORNING PEP TALKS

IS IT IMPORTANT

Your focus this week is on **prioritizing things in your life.**

Some of you may know that I'm getting married in a few weeks. Everything feels like a bit of a whirlwind with the final details coming together.

Some of my friends have thought I was ten shades of crazy because most of the details haven't been that important to me. I've said from the beginning the things I cared the most about are: good food (y'all know I love to eat), beautiful pictures, and a meaningful ceremony... oh and you know I want to look good too! But everything else, I literally, I don't care too much about.
Flowers.
Decorations.
Favors.
Dresses.

Listen, it's not that these things aren't valuable, they just aren't top of my list of things I'm choosing to invest too much time, money or energy into.

It's been a bit of a challenge because I actually DO have to give them some energy, but goodness I could almost just show up and be surprised by these details and probably be just as happy.

It's interesting to me because people assume everything has to be **so important** when it's your wedding. People are shocked when I say "I don't care about (insert some detail)."

But, much like with life, everything can't be of equal importance.

The biggest question I ask myself: Is it important or is it just filler?

If it's important. Go for it. Pour your energy and resources into it. Make progress.

If it's filler. Bump it down a notch. Watch the amount of energy you're investing into it. If you have the extra resources, then move forward. If not, it's okay.

Your challenge this week: Ask yourself, Is it Important or Just Filler?

Do this for every task you have on your schedule. See where you may be wasting some valuable

resources on filler that you could be putting towards something of importance.

Listen, if you want to live an incredible life, and do all the fun and amazing things you dream of doing, it starts with making things a priority.

xoxo---

Colene

PS--- Sending you lots of great energy this week!

LOVE
YOURSELF
ENOUGH

MONDAY MORNING PEP TALKS

LOVE YOURSELF ENOUGH

Your focus this week is on **Loving Yourself enough...**

This week is the week of love. Yes, I know that Valentine's Day is a super commercial holiday, but I'm a sucker for love. And I love LOVE in all kinds.

What I have learned, is regardless of my relationship status, I know it's more important to love myself!

Love yourself enough:
- to be honest about what you really want.
- to laugh loudly.
- to take care of your body
- to rest before you burnout
- to learn something new
- to schedule the doctor's appointments
- to put your phone away
- to ask for help
- to treat yourself
- to take a nap

- to trust your gut
- to say no
- to say yes to something exciting
- to cry it out
- to dance in your car
- to tell someone how they hurt you
- to spend a day doing nothing
- to spend the day getting sh*t done
- to drink more water
- to own your truth
- to use your voice
- to up level your life
- to buy the good stuff
- to save for your future
- to be uncomfortable
- to be exactly who you want to be!

The most important person to develop a healthy, loving relationship with is yourself. So this week, while everyone is talking about romance and relationships, give yourself a little more TLC.

Your challenge this week: Every day do something to show yourself some love.

Love comes in all forms, and just in case no one tells you enough... I love you, and am so happy you're here!

xoxo---

Colene

ASK YOUR

INNER CHILD

MONDAY MORNING PEP TALKS

ASK YOUR INNER CHILD

Hey _____-

Your focus this week is on **Asking Your Inner Child.**

There's something about a birthday that makes you become a bit more reflective. My birthday is this week, and every year, the second February rolls around, I start to do an inventory of my life.

What's working?
What's not working?
What do I wish I did more of?
What do I wish I did less of?

Not just for the year, but collectively in my thirty-some years.

This year, my biggest takeaway was to trust my inner child more.

When I look at pictures of my younger self, girlfriend knew what was up!

Young Colene had fun at every turn.
Young Colene loved to wear fun outfits and accessories.
Young Colene laughed... really loudly.
Young Colene was SO confident in everything she did.
Young Colene just twirled around like she owned the world.

She wasn't bogged down with "cant's". She didn't care what other people thought. She wasn't nervous or anxious. She didn't have any stories stuck in her head about who she was besides being amazing.

Young Colene followed joy like a guiding light!

Your younger self knows who you are at the core.
Your younger self only sees the best parts of you.
Your younger self is waiting for you to remember who you were before anyone told you you couldn't.

Your challenge this week: Ask Your Inner Child for guidance.

Use this week to try to follow your inner child instead of doing what you always do. Have fun with this! You need it!

xoxo---

Colene

WELCOME THE NEW

MONDAY MORNING PEP TALKS

WELCOME THE NEW

Hi there---

Your focus this week is on **<u>Welcoming the New.</u>**

It's almost spring. Time changed. I'm getting married this week!

It seems like I just told you all that I got engaged (it's was a year and a half ago), and now the week is here for me to get married.

I'm excited! But, just like with anything new, I feel a sense of the unknowns... if you let it, it can totally turn you into a wonky person.

So instead, I'm choosing to focus my energy on welcoming in the new in my life.

I studied Anthropology (no, not the store.)in college...

One of the things that I found the most fascinating was that regardless of culture, we all have certain rites of passage that mark a change in identity.

Birth. Puberty. Education. Marriage. Death.

Every culture does something different, but it all follows the same route: Separation. Transition. Incorporation.

I love that we have ways to transition from one stage of life to the next... from the old to the new!

The problem is that many times, we don't take the time to embrace the transition. Outside of the big ones, we tend to move from one phase to the next without much thought, reflection, or intention.

If you've ever felt like you may be holding on to something, odds are you didn't give yourself the space and energy to transition fully.

So, your goal this week is to focus on welcoming the new.

What is something new in your life? It can be big or small.
What did you have to give up, or change in order to get it? This is a key part of the transition!
Who did you become?
What's good about this new you?

Tell me what your last transition was!

Have a great week!

xoxo---

Colene

Colene H. Elridge

SIMPLE WINS

MONDAY MORNING PEP TALKS

SIMPLE WINS

I don't know about you, but I know that while I enjoy the simple things in life, my brain loves to overcomplicate everything!

It's constantly trying to convince me that things can't be THAT simple and that I need to add 15 more steps, 3 more processes, and 25 more layers of confusion.

Somehow, we start to believe that if something is too simple, it's not good enough. We also start to believe that complex equals greatness.

I remember I was once on a diet and I would look at recipes and think, "Oh! This looks fancy!" or "I bet I'd LOVE this". Then, I'd have to go buy all these odd ingredients that by the time I actually had to fix the food, I would be so overwhelmed with the recipe, that I wouldn't make it. My best weeks were when I would make ground beef and

baked chicken, and an assortment of mixed veggies.

Super simple!
Super easy!
Super effective!

The thing is, most things in life are really simple. Or, I guess I should say, most things CAN be really simple.

When you choose to complicate things (remember everything is a choice), you are giving away your energy. You know, the life force that helps you get things done...

What I have found over and over again, especially in business, is **Simple Wins**! Literally, the things I've had the most success with in life have been a result of keeping it simple and without overwhelm.

This week, your focus is on keeping it super simple! I mean, how can you make something even simpler than it already is?

Check your routines.
Check your work.
Check your schedule.
Check your wardrobe.
Check everything.

Make it simple!

Your energy is depending on you!

Simply Yours,

Colene

PS--- If you have to pick one area of your life to keep complex, I suggest ice cream flavors! HA! :)

I DID IT
MY WAY

MONDAY MORNING PEP TALKS

I DID IT MY WAY

I met with a client last week who is trying to expand her business. As we were talking she starts to tell me what everyone else in her field is doing.

"Well, so and so has a two-part training. And, so and so does this online."

She was telling me everything everyone else was doing, and I looked at her and said, "I don't care what everyone else is doing, what I care about is what do YOU WANT to do"?

She looked at me blankly... then said, "I don't know."

Now, here's the truth... she does know what she wants. She was too scared to say it.

The world is full of copies. You can look at what everyone else is doing and it's easy to think

copying them will get you the same success. But, all you'll end up with is an unauthentic version of yourself.

Learn from people.
See what they're doing.
Figure out what works for you.
Make it your own.

Learn to disrupt not duplicate.

<u>Your focus this week is on doing things your way.</u>
Do something creative. Do something new. Don't just do it the way everyone else is doing it. Add your own flair to it!

The way that you stand out (at work, in life, online, in organizations, etc.) is to add value by doing things differently. You are an original masterpiece... let's show the world that your value is in your uniqueness. Your value is how you see the world. Your value is in your voice.

How can you do things your own way this week?

With Appreciation---

Colene

SETTLING VS. CHOOSING

MONDAY MORNING PEP TALKS

SETTLING VS. CHOOSING

I see it all the time... you walk around from day to day doing whatever it is you do on Mondays and the next thing you know it's a new year, a new decade, a new stage of life.

How did this happen?

How did you trick yourself to believe that this is the life you chose for yourself?

I'll tell you how, you settled...

Somewhere along the way you told yourself that this was "good enough".
You told yourself that you were safe and comfortable, and that's all that mattered.
You let the fear of the unknown stop you from jumping head-first into something new.
You played small.
You dimmed your own light.

You made excuses.
You settled into a life that was never meant for you!

And the next thing you know, you have a life that's not like the one you imagined for yourself.

That's okay! Because today is your wake-up call!

Listen, friend... you get one life!

ONE!

Don't keep settling into the life that not what you want.

Fight with everything you've got to make your choice the one that creates the life you desire... the life you dream about... the life you deserve!

Choose to show up for yourself.
Choose how you want to feel throughout the day.
Choose the legacy you want to leave.
Choose the work you do.
Choose your goals over someone else's.
Choose to shine bright without being embarrassed.
Choose to want abundance in all areas of your life.
Choose to do the work, instead of allowing excuses.
Choose to do hard things.
Choose to make empowered decisions.
Choose boundaries.
Choose action.
Choose you!

Whatever that looks like for you is perfect! You don't have to justify it to anyone... but don't sell yourself short by not giving it a shot!

So, are you settling or choosing?

This week, your focus is on admitting areas in your life that you are settling, and make a decision to choose something different.

With Appreciation---

Colene

LESSONS FROM AN ORANGE

MONDAY MORNING PEP TALKS

LESSONS FROM AN ORANGE

I was on a call with a client last week, and she asked me how I stay so calm. I kinda laughed, because while I'm calm most of the time, I have my moments of freaking out too. But, I tend to prioritize my emotional health more than anything.

While I think all emotions are necessary and valid, and that there are no bad emotions, there are emotions that I don't want to carry around with me all the time. I know some emotions, when not properly expressed can damage relationships and drain my energy.

I was reminded of this story that the late Wayne Dyer told. He tells it far better than I, so I'm going to use his words:

I was preparing to speak at an "I Can Do It" conference and I decided to bring an orange on stage with me as a prop for my lecture. I opened a

I hope if you find that you don't like what's coming out, that you take some time to figure out the source. Then replace it with something you like better.

With Appreciation---

Colene

Colene H. Elridge

BE THE
WEIRDEST
PERSON YOU
KNOW

MONDAY MORNING PEP TALKS

BE THE WEIRDEST PERSON YOU KNOW

I have a few things to tell you:

1. I like to eat baked beans with potato salad... Like mixed together.

2. I love to pick random hairs and bumps on my husband. Dr. Pimple Popper is one of my favorite YouTube channels. (Warning: do not look up if you're squeamish.)

3. I got attuned (basically certified) to give Reiki. It's a Japanese relaxation technique that involves moving energy. I've benefited from Reiki for years, so I'm thankful that I can share it with other people. Though it's not a service I currently offer, it will someday be apart of what I do.

4. I tend to find myself in really random and awkward situations... I once hiked an off-the-beaten-path trail to see the Golden Gate Bridge with my Uber Driver. As we were hiking up, I

remember thinking, "How did I end up here taking random pictures with my Uber driver?" I wish this was a one-time occurrence, but things like this happen to me all the time.

5. You know how they say find something that makes you want to jump out of bed in the morning? I love the work that I do, and I am so inspired by it, but I really love sleep. Most of the time the main motivation for getting up in the morning is the bathroom calling my name.

Listen, I could go on and one about my oddities, and the random things about myself, but I don't want to bore you. Sometimes, we feel like if someone knew just how weird we are, they would judge us, and no longer like us. But, what I have found is that the more you let people know who you are... I mean the real you, the more connection you'll find!

Don't make apologies for the things that make you, you! Be the weirdest person you know!

<u>Your goal this week is to share something slightly odd about yourself with someone.</u> Let it out! Use this as a way to build a better relationship. The world wants to see all of you, not just the parts you think are pretty enough to share. I'd love to hear something about you, if you'd like to share! :)

With Appreciation---

Colene

A CHANGE WILL DO YOU GOOD

MONDAY MORNING PEP TALKS

A CHANGE WILL DO YOU GOOD

Your focus this week is on embracing change.

I do a lot of work with organizations in the midst of change. It never fun for anyone to acknowledge that it's uncomfortable, but goodness it is. But change is also a gift.

What change do you know is inevitable in your life?

What makes the thought of change so challenging?

Did you know, that regardless of the actual change, you get to decide if it's gonna be easy or hard? Cause you do!

Think about a change you've made… what made it successful? I imagine mindset played a big role in it.

Whatever it is, now's **the perfect time to embrace change.**

When you make the choice to embrace change, you make life even easier. Stop resisting!

I've been there. I've been scared to make changes in my career, life, and business… but what I've found is that when I embrace it, step out of my comfort zone, and dive in, it's had the greatest impact on my life.

There is NO change in your comfort zone, y'all… You gotta make a little step to see what's out there.

<u>Your homework this week is to make a change with intention.</u> It doesn't matter what the change is. Don't overthink it! Just make it happen. The more you're committed to your change, the easier it becomes a part of the norm. _

You're ready, friend!

Have a great week!
xoxo-

Colene

IT'S A _____
STATE OF
MIND

MONDAY MORNING PEP TALKS

IT'S A _____ STATE OF MIND

<u>Your focus this week is on resiliency.</u>

If you're like me, you probably read the title and started singing Billy Joel's <u>New York State of Mind,</u> but that's not what we're talking about today. We are talking mindset.

If there's <u>one variable to your success</u> that you have any control over it's this… your mindset!

Your life, career, business, relationships, everything is a direct reflection of your mindset.

When we get discouraged it's hard to spot opportunity let alone act on it. Now, I'm not saying be a Pollyanna and bury your head in the sand, but what can you find positive about any situation.

I'll never forget taking this class in college about the connection between health, healing, and the mind. There was a study that showed people with

illness that thought they had a positive prognosis had a higher recovery rate than people who thought negatively. Your thoughts can literally save your life.

Notice this week where your state of mind is at:

Are you **feeling hopeful** or have you given up?

Are you **seeing fresh possibility** in your life or do things look stale and like they won't change?

Are you getting **new insights and ideas** and acting on them or are you stuck spinning on the same downward spiral of Debbie-downer thoughts?

Don't buy into negative thoughts , the only importance they have is what you give them.

Wherever you're at right now you're just one thought away from an even better experience , just one thought away from becoming resilient and turning things around

Have a great week!

xoxo-

Colene

A-C-T-I-O-N

MONDAY MORNING PEP TALKS

A-C-T-I-O-N

Your focus this week is on ACTION.

Too often it's easy to find yourself **lost in the process** rather than taking action steps towards creating what you want.

Don't over think your:

"How to"?
"What if"?
"Why me"?

Or anything else your spinning on right now....

Instead **consider what you can do today,** however small, even just one step to move you closer to your desire becoming REAL.

It's not always about your mindset, sometimes, what's key is that you take an action step regardless.

<u>Your homework this week is to take action on a goal you have every single day.</u>

What action are you taking this week?

Have a great week!

xoxo-

Colene

NO MORE DRAMA

MONDAY MORNING PEP TALKS

NO MORE DRAMA

Your focus this week is on **being drama free.**

If the last few months of the ramped-up election cycle has taught me anything, it's that we love drama! Everything is a show, and we are just observers. Everything makes the headlines, and everyone on social media has an opinion. Drama is fine for your reality tv show addiction (no judgement, I'm hooked on 90 Day Finance), but not good for our everyday lives.

What I've seen lots of time is just before we're about to up level our career or lives in a big way we are great at creating extra drama. We have arguments that aren't necessary, we manifest illness, we do things that directly (or indirectly) sabotage our progress.

Progress can be scary, especially if you're creating more abundance in your life, or stepping into your greatness. I think staying stagnant is scarier, but it tends to be far more comfortable.

Drama Free Zone

This week, create a drama free zone. Set an intention that your life will be drama free and create space to keep it that way. We like to give away our control in this area of our lives, but remember it's not about what's happening, it's about how you respond. Choose to respond without the drama.

Save the drama for your mama! :)

Have a great week!

xoxo-

Colene

DECISION DETOX

MONDAY MORNING PEP TALKS

DECISION DETOX

Your focus this week is on **limiting decision fatigue.**

As you're reading this, my guy and I are heading to Las Vegas. I'm going for a conference where Tony Robbins and Richard Branson are speaking, and my guy decided to tag along. A little bit business, a little bit vacation, a little bit personal development, sounds like a WIN!

As we were planning our trip, I was overwhelmed with the amount of decisions that needed to be made. There are literally 1500 hotels in Vegas, and which one should we stay at? Do we need to stay on the Strip or should we just visit the Strip? Should we splurge one night and get a crazy expensive room, or just keep it simple? What day should we leave? What airline should we fly? Should we stay an extra day, or come back early? Should we get a rental car?

So many decisions!

As I found myself in the middle of decision hell, I had to force myself to limit my decisions. Everything didn't need to be over-analyzed. Everything didn't need 18 hours of thought, and everything would probably be okay if I just made A decision, versus being stuck with a million decision.

That place where you feel stuck is what some scientist call "decision fatigue". You have a limited amount of energy throughout the day, and do you really want to expend so much of yours just making decisions?

In a matter of an hour, I booked the hotel and the flights. When I called my guy to tell him where we would be staying, he said, "It's actually my favorite hotel on the Strip". (Score one for me!) I felt an instant wave of relief.

When we are overwhelmed with too many decisions, it can take its toll on us mentally, physically and emotionally. Since I know we're all smart, successful women, I'm not suggesting burying your head in the sand and never making a decision. Decisions can be where the magic happens.

What I am suggesting is not letting decision making weigh you down to the point of indecisiveness.

Sometimes making a decision doesn't have to be that hard.

Decision Detox

This week, I want you to experiment with a Decision Detox. (Don't worry, this isn't as painful as that time you decided to do that juice detox.) Pick an area of your life where you are giving yourself too many options. Example: Should I get up at 5:30 to do yoga, or get up and write? Should I wear a dress or pants today? Should I pack a lunch, or just run out and grab something? You can see all these things require a decision, which means they require energy.

For this week, limit the amount of decisions you make by just doing. For example, if you're asking yourself if you should do yoga or write, just say "This week, I'll get up at 5:30 and write". Then do it.

Would love to hear where you're decision detoxing!

Limited choices in your day can lead to limitless freedom in your life!

Have a great week!

xoxo-

Colene

MORE THAN WORDS

MONDAY MORNING PEP TALKS

MORE THAN WORDS

Your focus this week is on your **word.**

One of my favorite books is <u>The Four Agreements</u> by Don Miguel Ruiz. If you've been around here for awhile, you've heard me talk about it before.

Essentially, Ruiz points to four agreements that can help us succeed in and enjoy life.

The first is: **"Be impeccable with your word".**

What he means by this is not about keeping your word or saying the right words but rather **being impeccable with how you speak to and about yourself.**

It is believed that life and death is determined by how we speak to and about ourselves.

Meaning, your words matter... A LOT! Your words become actions, and your actions become your life.

So, this week **be impeccable with your word towards yourself.**

Don't let negative thoughts or fear keep a hold of you a second longer.

Don't believe everything you tell yourself, especially, if you're not in a place of love.

Be gentle, be kind, be easy with your word.

Have a great week!

xoxo-

Colene

TAKE
IT
EASY

MONDAY MORNING PEP TALKS

TAKE IT EASY

Your focus this week is on **being okay exactly where you're at**.

You have t**he ability to enjoy life a**nd feel fulfilled right now, *regardless of your circumstances.*

Now I know this may sound CRAZY, especially if your bank account is empty, you don't feel far enough ahead in your career and you're not happy with your image, marriage or (insert other).

But hear me out... Except for your expectations and thoughts around **what should and shouldn't be happening by now**, not to mention all that **self criticism and judgement** you're putting on yourself and others, **you'd actually be happy and feel fulfilled.**

It's how we're wired when we're not lost in thought.

So, this week, I want **you to ditch your expectations, wants and needs,** and instead **live your life <u>with no preferences.</u>**

(This coming from the woman who was once had a lot of "requirements" to be happy)

See **how much fun life actually gets when you're in deep appreciation for wherever you are** and whatever you've got.

Enjoy your week!

xoxo-

Colene

PS- One of my FAVORITE quotes from the book <u>A Course in Miracles</u> says, "Those who are certain of the outcome can afford to wait and wait without anxiety." It's always such a reminder for me that everything is happening exactly as it should be!

CHECK YES OR NO

MONDAY MORNING PEP TALKS

CHECK YES OR NO

This week's focus is on **making a decision with ease.**

My guy always ask me where I want to go eat. While it's sweet that he's (in theory) trying to be considerate, it's always just one more decision to make during the day.

Are you worn out? Are you making too many decisions during your day?

Do I want oatmeal or toast?
Do I want to wash my hair this morning or wait until tomorrow?
Do I hit the snooze or jump up?
Should I wear the green dress or the red dress?

Decision. Decisions. Decision.

On average we make 35,000 decisions a day. **35,000!** Yet, everything doesn't need to be a tough decision.

When faced with so many decisions in a day, we can have decision fatigue. That leads to poor

decision making... Note: that's sometimes how I end up eating ice cream for dinner.

So, what can you do?

Limit the decisions and/or limit the energy you spend making decisions.

My one top trick is if I'm indifferent to the outcome of the decision, meaning I'm feeling okay either way, I'll literally flip a coin to make the decision. Depending on the outcome of the flip, I can learn a lot about how I really feel...

If I feel disappointed in the outcome, I know which way I need to go.
If I feel excited about the outcome, I know which way I need to go.
If I still feel indifferent about the outcome, the decision has been made for me.

See how easy that is?

This week, your goal is to limit the number of decisions you make.

See how many decisions you make with ease...

Have a great week!

xoxo-

Colene

WHISTLE WHILE YOU WORK

MONDAY MORNING PEP TALKS

WHISTLE WHILE YOU WORK

This week's focus is on **finding purpose in your work.**

One of the reasons I started writing these Monday Morning Pep Talks was the dread I have felt about going to work either in an environment that wasn't supportive, or in a job that didn't feel meaningful. The dread that starts to creep in Sunday night... you know, where you start to weigh the thought of not going to work on Monday?

But, you drag yourself out of bed and show up. You make it through the day, and keep praying for Friday to show up.

This is not a life! You deserve more than this!

You may think, "If I could get a new job, THEN I'd be happy."

The truth is, you don't necessarily need a new job... you need to connect to your purpose. Jobs come and go, but finding your purpose and your passion can change a job, your attitude and your life.

Can you imagine going to work every day feeling excited about the work you get to do? Can you imagine knowing you're doing the work that is in line with your purpose? Can you imagine feeling fully satisfied at the end of the day?

This is possible! Even if you're currently in a job you hate, you can still find purpose.

This week, your goal is to find purpose in your work.

How can you start to tie the work you're currently doing into something of purpose? What are you learning from your current work? What do you like about your current work? What do you want to be different? Who are you serving? What difference are you making?

Start answering these questions...

There is meaning in everything.

Have a great week!

xoxo-

Colene

BE

HERE

MONDAY MORNING PEP TALKS

BE HERE

Your focus this week is on **Being Here... Now.**

It's easy to get distracted... There is an alert from Facebook, or Twitter, or Instagram. You get a text message. You get emails. Commercials. Phone calls. Doorbell rings!

In a world where everyone's vying for your attention, it's completely up to you where you focus your attention, and where you choose to give your time and energy.

At the beginning of most of my workshops, I ask people if they are "All In"... meaning are you ready to be present for our time together? Are you committed to giving your attention to just one thing in this moment? You'd be surprised how much more you can learn without distractions.

This week, your task is to focus on Being Here... Now. I want you to be mindful about what you give your attention to as well as how you spread your energy. Make sure you're happy with where your attention is going. If not, make a quick change.

Enjoy your week,

xoxo-

Colene

PS--- Can I just tell you how thankful I am for you?!?! Have an outstanding week! :)

PLEASE LET ME FEEL INNER PEACE

MONDAY MORNING PEP TALKS

PLEASE LET ME FEEL INNER PEACE

This week, your challenge is to **focus on finding Inner Peace.**

There are lots of things in the world that you can not control. You can't make anyone else handle a situation exactly the same way you would. You can't control your boss. You can't control someone being insensitive. You can't control the news. You can't control a loved one getting sick. You can't control a lot of things that happen in life...

You can control your thoughts and you can maintain your peace.

Over the past few weeks, it seems a lot of people I know are having some life challenges. Some major, some small, all enough to make us feel a sense of uneasiness.

The challenge in these times is to find your own inner peace. (Even if just for a moment.)

What brings you peace in times of frustration?

I want to share with you a song that's renewed my strength in finding my own peace, and the inspiration for this week's Pep Talk. It's called <u>Inner Peace</u> and is performed by Beautiful Chorus.

The lyrics are simple:
"Please let me feel inner peace.
From my center. At the center of me.
My heart is open. I am aware. In me's a knowing of love love love."

Wanna hear it? Yes, you do. You can find it on Youtube. I promise it will make you feel a bit more peace during your day.

Your peace is a gift. Your peace is your right. Your peace is the source of all the good you will put into the world.

Let peace begin with you!

xoxo---

Colene

ALIGNMENT BEFORE ACTION

MONDAY MORNING PEP TALKS

ALIGNMENT BEFORE ACTION

This week your challenge is to **find alignment before action.**

I've been doing a lot of research lately on people who seem to excel at life... top performers, and achievement. One of the main reason is I'm fascinated by what makes people tick, and how (not necessarily why) people achieve. The phrase that keeps coming up in every piece I've read is this...

Alignment BEFORE Action.

It seems that the top performers all tend to do this one thing to achieve more than most. They get SUPER clear on what they want their outcome to be before they take one step.

Here's an example: Average Person Sending Email An average person sits down, quickly writes an email, scans for errors, and then hits send.

A High-Performer Sending Email
A high-performer will sit and ask what is the
purpose of this email, what do they want the
individual to feel when they read this email, what
outcome would they like from this email, and how
can they be proactive in achieving those results
BEFORE they send the email.

Both send emails, both get results, odds are the
high-performer gets better results from an email
that took maybe 2-3 minutes longer to send.

The idea is to get clear on what you want before
you start to take action. I do this in some areas of
my life, but not in all. It's something I'm personally
trying to get better at. It's like sharpening a saw
before you try to cut a tree. If you take the time to
make sure your saw is sharp, you'll cut the tree
with more ease and less effort.

So, here is the first way that we go wrong. We think
that it is purely our action that creates. Yes, sure
action does produce results, but if this is all you
focus on, you are missing one key component –

Energy.

It is the energy behind the action that creates, not
just the action itself. This the key to the alignment
before action.

So, here is how you change that.

Take your focus off action, and put your focus on alignment first. You must bring your energy into alignment with what you want FIRST and then from there you take action.

How do you know you are IN alignment?

You know you are in alignment when you think about your outcome and you feel: Belief. Expectation. Knowing. Happiness. Excitement. Love. Joy. Certainty.

How do you know you are OUT of alignment?

You know you are out of alignment when you think about your outcome and you feel: Fear. Doubt. Worry. Anxiety. Frustration. Powerlessness.

So, this week, let's work on this together. Pick one area of your life that you want to focus on. Then think about how you can find alignment before taking action.

Sharpen the saws!

xoxo---

Colene

BE
BOLD

MONDAY MORNING PEP TALKS

BE BOLD

This week your challenge is to **Be Bold!**

Hello from 10,000 feet in the air. As I write this, I'm flying home from an amazing experience in San Diego, where I got the chance to speak at a conference called BOLD. I never take for granted to chances I have to speak to people and give them tips on creating Better Work + Better Life.

This conference inspired me to make some BOLD moves, and that's what I would love for you to focus on this week.

What does it mean to be BOLD?

Bold, by definition means showing the ability to take risks, and being confident and courageous.

What can you do to be BOLD this week?

Wear something that makes you feel confident. The bright red lipstick that you feel sexy, but it makes you stand out a little more than you usually like.

Be honest with someone you love about what you need in your relationship.

Put in your resignation from the job that's sucking your soul... but try to have something else lined up.

Sleep for 8 hours, and wake up feeling rejuvenated... That's truly something BOLD!

Speak up when you see something that is wrong.

Start the workout program you've wanted to start, but felt embarrassed to start.

Y'all, **make a BOLD move this week**. Do something that makes you feel empowered, energized, and full of life!

When you start making one BOLD move it's easier to make another one. And another one. And another one.

Be BOLD!!!

xoxo---

Colene

TAP INTO YOUR JEALOUSY

MONDAY MORNING PEP TALKS

TAP INTO YOUR JEALOUSY

I spent most of my Sunday afternoon riding in a car, actively stalking people on Instagram who were invited to Oprah's house for her Super Soul Sunday Brunch. My fascination quickly turned to pangs of jealousy...

Why does she get to do something so cool?
How did he get invited?

Hmmmmm... They aren't really saying anything that interesting.

As I was actively complaining to my guy about this, he looked at me and said, "Colene, you're just as good as anyone there. You just don't know it yet."

[side note] So, this is part of why I love this guy... he has his faults like everyone else, but he's an encourager!

His words stopped me in my tracks. And instead of being jealous that I wasn't there, I started to think about what I could learn from the people who were there...

What are they doing right?
What could I start doing?

Here's a bit of truth... if you feel jealous of someone, there is something you can learn from them. There is something that they have, or do, that a part of you wants. Don't let jealousy drive your actions, let learning drive your actions.

Your focus this week is to **tap into your jealousy.** Figure out the root of it, then flip the script.

And just so you know, I always have to remind myself that I am on my own journey. Comparing myself to anyone, especially someone who is not me, is stealing all my joy!

You're on your own journey too. Learn, grow, and do you!

xoxo---

Colene

FORGIVE AGAIN

MONDAY MORNING PEP TALKS

FORGIVE AGAIN

Can I tell you something, forgiveness is hard.

Like sometimes, it doesn't seem worth it.

If you've been around Coach Colene land for awhile, you know a couple of years ago, I set out on a journey to forgive my father. He committed suicide when I was young and it has been this road to empathy, acceptance, and forgiveness. The journey has lead me to unexpected results, and the kind of awareness that I never knew existed.

Three years ago, when I finally forgave my father, I thought that was the end. However, what I have found was that was just the beginning. You see forgiveness isn't something that is always a one-time thing.

Last week, my heart broke for a friend who lost the father of her daughters to suicide. Surprisingly to me, this stirred up a wave of emotions within me. I was sad for my friend. I was sad for her daughters. I was sad for their father. I was sad for the families involved.

And then, out of nowhere, I was hit with the pangs of anger. Anger that I could relate to those poor girls. Anger that I know that for the rest of their lives, they will question why. Anger that one day they will get married (as I soon am), and feel the pain of not having their father there to walk them down the aisle. Anger that I had to think about this AGAIN... dang it! I'm tired of having to think about this!

So, I found myself in a space to forgive again. Here's what I know... anger doesn't serve me well. In fact, it doesn't look good on me at all! It doesn't make me feel good. And, I truly don't like having that pit in my stomach that my anger resides in.

So, I worked through it again. I reminded myself of my father's pain and feelings of helplessness. I reminded myself, that everything in my life has taught me valuable lessons, including this. I reminded myself that I became resilient, strong, and loving. I reminded myself that I can extend compassion and grace to everyone and it might save their life. I reminded myself that every step in my journey hasn't been by accident, but all a part of a greater purpose. I reminded myself that I am thankful to him for everything that he's given me, including life. Half of me is made up of him, and I'm thankful for that. I reminded myself that I loved him... truly loved him for the time he was able to love me.

There were lots of tears. There were moments of feelings of heartbreak all over again. There were moments that it felt hard.

And then, there was the great moment of release.

So, before we move into a new year, I want you to think about who you need to forgive. What do you need to let go of? How can apply more empathy to the situation? How can you forgive yourself?

I don't care what the situation is... forgive them for yourself. You don't have to excuse the behavior. You don't have to become besties with the person or have an ongoing relationship. All you need to do is let go of the pain, anger, frustration, hurt and move into a place of forgiveness, empathy, and love.

I don't want to make it seem like it's always easy. It's not. But, it's always worth it.

<u>This week, your focus is on forgiveness</u>. Don't drag this into 2018. I promise you it's weighing you down and stopping you from reaching your best self.

xoxo---

Colene

PS--- Suicide is never the answer. If you need help, please call the National Suicide Prevention Hotline: 800-273-8255.

HAPPY NEW YEAR

MONDAY MORNING PEP TALKS

HAPPY NEW YEAR

I'm so grateful to start the New Year with you!

The beginning of a new year is such an exciting time – the countdown, the champagne toast, the silly hats, the midnight kiss, the fireworks, the sparkles and glitz – it's all so magical! I love that it's tradition to celebrate the possibility that lies ahead in the year to come. **As you know, I'm all about believing anything is possible!**

In my mind, the new year is the perfect opportunity for setting intentions for the year ahead – hence all the resolution making.

But how often have you made a New Year's resolution, only to see that resolution fall by the wayside after just a couple of weeks? I think most everyone's experienced that at some point.
So right now, I have a little insight to share to help you set intentions for the new year and

actually keep them – so that you can reach your goals this year.
1. Give it time.
2. Stop dabbling.
3. See it daily.

Give it time--- did you know it takes an average of 66 days to create a new habit? 66 days! After 66 days it doesn't seem as hard to do... it starts to feel more natural.

When I heard this for the first time, I flashed back to all the moments when I didn't follow through – **and it all started to make sense!**

The truth is, as much as I had wanted to make a change, I didn't give it enough time to stick.

Maybe you can relate?

Stop Dabbling--- listen, I don't want to be too hard on you, but you've got to stop dabbling and expecting results. You've got to be all in! Dabbling will not get you where you want to be. Dabbling won't get you to the outcomes you want. Dabbling will leave you right where you've always been.

See it daily--- I encourage you to write your intentions daily... yes, every single day, write them out with pen and paper. Why? Where your energy goes, so does your intention. So, give your intentions some energy every single day. It literally

takes you 1-2 minutes, but it will start you off on the right foot.

I also love to use my vision board as a visual reminder of what I'm working towards.

So think about what you want to change and implement this year.

Maybe for you it's a new powerful morning routine. (I recommend meditation.)

Maybe you want to go to a new yoga studio every day.

Maybe you want to work less in your business and delegate.

Maybe you want to try cutting sugar out of your diet. (Hello, ME!)

Regardless of the goal, I encourage you to give these tips a try.

Now, your mind may try to tell you that your goals aren't possible, or that your new thought habits are too hard or unnatural. When that happens, just remember to feel the feelings that come up, and then operate from a place of knowledge that although your mind may be resisting this change – and it's probably resisting getting outside your comfort zone – **you can flip the switch on those thoughts and refocus on your goals.**

You have what it takes! You can do anything if you simply put your mind to it (and by the way, it also helps to schedule it into your calendar or set reminders on your phone)!

Truly, there is so much potential for you in the year to come – so no more dabbling, friend! Now is the perfect time to put new practices in place to help you move forward toward your dreams this year, and to make them stick. After all, your dreams are in your heart for a reason.

Make this year your year to make those dreams your reality!

xoxo---

Colene

BOUNDARIES, A RADICAL ACT OF SELF LOVE

MONDAY MORNING PEP TALKS

BOUNDARIES... A RADICAL ACT OF SELF-LOVE

Your focus this week is on **Creating Boundaries Without Guilt.**

This week we're talking boundaries!

Last week I found myself in a situation where I had to set a stronger, clearer defined boundary with someone I really like and respect.

Y'all it was rough. I cried afterwards. I actually went to the bathroom and got sick afterwards... and then I cried.

You see, what I realized is that when I set a boundary, I think it's rational, practical, and out of a place of love and mutual respect.

What others sometimes feel is threatened, hurt, and like you're assailing a personal attack on their character.

Both feelings are valid, yet, I truly don't care how **my** boundaries make **them** feel. Not to say I don't care about them. I care so much about them that I want us both to be happy in this relationship. I didn't particularly set them for them, I set them for me.

I've not always been good at boundaries. In fact, I've been really bad with it in the past. I didn't want to disappoint people. I wanted people to like me. I worried if I stirred the pot a little too much, they would think I was an overly emotional woman.

Now…
I still don't want to disappoint people, but their disappointment is not my issue.
I still want people to like me, but feel comfortable if I make them uncomfortable too.
I still might be overly emotional (my feelings have feelings, HA), but my ability to feel deeply makes me who I am.

Boundaries are positive. They create healthier relationships (in all forms).

Here are my tips on creating better boundaries:
1. **Be clear on what you want.**
Don't be wishy-washy on your boundary. Let the person know exactly what the line is, and what the consequence is for crossing the line.

1. **Make sure your words match your actions.**

If your words don't match, you run the risk of sending mixed signals on what you actually expect.

1. **Be firm and consistent with your boundary.**

You may have to say your boundary several times for the person to understand what you want. Say it as many times as you feel comfortable. Assertive is NOT a bad word.

1. **Follow through if someone crosses a boundary.**

Don't just let someone cross your boundary without consequences. This is sometimes the hardest part.

1. **Approach with love.**

Every time I have to set a boundary, I remind myself I am doing this out of love: self-love and love for my relationship with that person.

Your action item this week is to see where can you set a better boundary in your life?

Start small. It's not always fun. It's not always easy. But it is certainly necessary. You owe this to yourself and to the future of your relationships.

xoxo---

Colene

Colene H. Elridge

HONOR
YOURSELF

MONDAY MORNING PEP TALKS

HONOR YOURSELF

One of my favorite recent books is <u>The Four Tendencies </u>by Gretchen Rubin. She says there are four major ways that we respond to expectations, and the people who fall into each category are, Rebels, Upholders, Obligers, and Questioners.

I'm an Obliger... 100% Obliger. Meaning, I respond really well to external expectations, but often not to internal expectations.

It's something I've struggled with my entire life. If I tell someone that I'll do something, I will, without question do it. I mean I have mastered the art of rallying to do things for other people...

BUT, if I tell myself that I will do something, it's super easy for me to come up with 1000 reasons why I need to wash my hair, clean the bathroom, or anything else to procrastinate. It's a constant internal battle.

But, the last couple of years, I've wanted to honor myself more.

Finish the things I start. Do the things I say I want to do.

So, I did some things to make that happen. I hired my own coach. I found layers of accountability in areas of my life that it's easy to slack in. I've built in additional support to make things happen.

The most important thing though, was I really started to honor myself more.

A commitment to myself is just as important as a commitment to anyone else. So, I work really hard to keep my word... to myself. My goals, my life, my future are too important for me not to.

Your goals, your life, and your future are important too.

So, this week, **your challenge is to honor yourself**.

Finish something you start. Do something, even if you don't feel like it. Meal prep your meals if you know it will make your life easier. Make your bed every morning. Simply, do the work.

Give yourself the gift of being fully committed to you!

Have a lovely week!

xoxo---

Colene

PS--- Take the quiz and let me know your
Tendency.

WHAT ARE YOU WAITING FOR?

MONDAY MORNING PEP TALKS

WHAT ARE YOU WAITING FOR?

For years my only dream was to be on Oprah. I would think, "If I could just meet Oprah, my life would be better." No joke! I thought about this often.

Every week, I would go on her show's website and check to see if there were any topics that I could be a guest for.

Nothing.
Nothing.
Nothing.

So, I kept longing for Oprah to call me. I kept thinking that if she would just call me, everything would change. I would get fit. I would get my sh*t together. I would drink more water... (you know I can't be dehydrated on Oprah's show.)

It was like my mind was just waiting for the permission to do all the things.

Then, a few years ago, through a series of crazy
events, I ended up in the same room as Oprah. I
was literally less than 20 feet away from her. With
an opportunity to introduce myself to her and ask a
question. I was so excited! I was ready! Then the
moment came, and...

I FROZE!
I couldn't move.
I broke out in a full-on sweat.
I couldn't talk.

My brother was literally trying to pick me up to get
me to fulfil my dream.

But, nothing!

Here's what I learned in that moment... It was
never about actually meeting Oprah. Don't get me
wrong, I'm still planning to actually meet and talk
to her someday.

It was about becoming the woman I needed to be to
meet Oprah.

I wasn't ready yet. If I had met Oprah then it would
have been a mess. I would have probably regretted
it because I would have come at it from a place of
thirstiness, instead of from a place of gratitude or
empowerment or strength.

I didn't need to meet Oprah to tell me that I was
worthy of becoming the woman I'm growing into
now... I needed myself to believe I was worthy of it.

Here's what I want you to know about your dreams... you have to become the person who is ready to receive those dreams. All of our dreams, regardless of what they are require another version of yourself. If it didn't we'd already have it.

So who do you need to become?

If you were to know that you could have exactly what you wanted today, what would you think? Would you be ready to receive it?

This week, your challenge is to identify one way you could get ready to receive your dreams. How can you step into the person you need to be? How can you stop waiting?

Oprah and I are rooting for you! :)

xoxo---

Colene

Colene H. Elridge

YOU CAN BE ANYTHING

MONDAY MORNING PEP TALKS

YOU CAN BE ANYTHING

I woke up early on Saturday morning to, as so many people did, watch the wedding of Prince Harry and Meghan Markle. I get sappy at weddings, but this wedding made me even more teary-eyed than normal. It started the second I saw Meghan riding in the car with her mother (I love good mother/daughter relationships), and random tears came and went for the next three hours.

Besides the obvious love themes of the day, my biggest takeaway is that you can be anything you want to be.

Yes, that sounds cheesy, but it's totally true. What do you think the odds were that Meghan Markle would marry an actual prince? I'd say those odds were bigger than the odds of you achieving your dream job, or starting a business, or learning a new skill, or anything else you dream of doing.

So, what if you just went for it?

What if you thought, if Meghan can get the fairy tale, so can I?

What if you decided that you wanted to see if, just possibly, your dreams could come true?

Because, why not you? There was nothing that makes Meghan Markle exceptionally different than you, and you, my friend, can totally be, do, or have whatever you're little heart desires.

What if you dreamed a little bigger? What if you thought outside the box? What if you created a life without limitations?

Be the queen in your own life! Hold your head up and walk into the week with the confidence that all your dreams are already coming true!

This week, your focus goal is to choose to be anything you want to be! Then take a second and close your eyes and see yourself living your dreams. Once you see it, you can make it happen! With Appreciation---

Colene

PS--- Did you watch the wedding? What was your favorite part?

BE
SEEN

MONDAY MORNING PEP TALKS

BE SEEN

A couple of weeks ago I spoke at a conference.

Normally when I speak, I try to go for the more casual route so that I can be more relatable to my audience (plus, it makes me less sweaty). But, for this conference, I knew I needed to dress up a bit more.

It was a conference of close to 400 professional women, and I didn't want to look like (as my mom would say) Joe Sh*t the rag man. Note: I thought Joe was an actual guy for most of my childhood, but that's another story.

Anyway, I went back and forth about what to wear, and I pulled out this yellow dress that I LOVE, but have only worn twice. It fits well. It looks good on me. But… it's bright yellow! It stands out! It's memorable. You can't just blend into the crowd with this dress on.

That morning, I went back and forth a few times about if I really wanted to wear this dress. I put on the dress and would change into a simple black dress. I'm not kidding, at least 5 times. Ultimately, I decided to wear the yellow dress!

You see, there's a point in your life where you have to **choose to be seen**. I mean, be seen in a big way!

Maybe it's wearing the yellow dress, or maybe it's speaking up during a business meeting.

Maybe it's doing a Facebook Live or posting a how-to video.

Maybe it's telling someone that you have a dream to be a professional baker, even though you work at a bank.

Whatever it is, be seen.

Somewhere along the lines we (especially women) were taught to not make a scene.

To be polite.

To blend into the background of life because if not… you're showy! Braggy. Too big for your britches (that's pants for those of y'all not from the south.)

So you did!

You did because it's super safe in the background. It's quiet. It's easy. I get it! But you were not born to play a background role in your own life. Be the lead!

This week, **I want you to make the intention to be seen every single day.**

Wear something that's a little too much.
Speak up without being called on.
Walk with a little more pep in your step.
Be seen this week.

What's your own yellow dress? Whatever you choose, I'd love to see! Share on social media and tag me in your post! (Instagram: @Coach_colene Facebook: Coach Colene) Or, email me and let me know. You n

See what it feels like to be the star in your life!

Xoxo---

Colene

BE
THE
CEO

MONDAY MORNING PEP TALKS

BE THE CEO

A few weeks ago I was teaching a workshop for a company experiencing big changes. I love working with organizations, because besides improving the lives of individuals, I have a great passion for improving workplaces. Call it the HR geek in me, but I truly love transforming organizations into "cultures of inclusion", a place where all employees feel valued, respected, and supported. We spend A LOT of time at work, and wouldn't it be great to work at a place where you feel valued every day? Respected on the basis that you are an employee within the organization? Supported to do your job? Yes. Yes. Yes.

During one of the workshops, a participant raised her hand and said, "Colene, that's great and all, but I don't have any power to make any changes. I'm just a [insert title here]."

I hate the word "just". "Just" implies limits. "Just" diminishes worth. "Just" is nothing more than an excuse to not do the work.

I called her on it.

I asked, "Do you mean to tell me that there is absolutely nothing you can do to improve the culture of your organization"? She responded with, "Well, I'm not the CEO, or even a director, what am I supposed to do"?

Here's a secret about leadership within organizations, yes, it's starts at the top, but the leaders who are there day in and day out making the workplaces better, often don't have a title to match. You don't have to be the president or CEO to lead effectively. In fact, and this is not to diminish the value of any CEO, but you can probably be a more effective leader if you're not the CEO.

The biggest misconception people have about leadership is the belief that leadership comes from having a position or title. There is a belief that you can't lead if you're not at the top. Leadership is not in position, it's in influence.

What I wanted this participant (and you) to understand is the person with the most influence is the one who wins. If you can gain influence amongst your peers, you will have genuine leadership, regardless of your title. You can lead others from anywhere in the organization, and

when you do, you make the organization better. Leadership is a choice you make, not an office you sit in. Anyone can choose to become a leader wherever he or she is. All of us have the ability to impact our workplaces for the positive.

So how do you do it?

You learn to develop your influence wherever you are in the organization by becoming holistic leader. You learn to lead in all directions (up, down, and across).

The best way to gain influence is through building relationships. I'm not suggesting you become BFFs with every person within your organizations, but I am suggesting you talk to people about stuff outside of the scope of their job.

WHAT?!?

Yes, I know it's shocking to remember that outside of the time you see your co-workers, they have actual lives, and do things with other people. Maybe, you could ask them about that. Show that you notice them as an individual as well.

Now, because I spent the greater part of my HR career investigating harassment complaints, I do want to offer this tiny disclaimer… Don't be creepy! Don't ask anything too personal. Don't cross the line.

Building relationships starts with communication. Building relationships at work also builds trust (something I think is missing in a lot of workplaces). Building relationships builds influence. Remember, (positive) influence = leadership.

So, the next time you think you don't have the power to change anything at work because you're "just" a [title], remember, you can always build influence, and you can always build relationships. Start where you are.

Your focus this week is to think of yourself as an influencer. How would you interact with your peers if you were already in a position of influence? Do that!!!

With Appreciation---

Colene

Colene H. Elridge

THIS ONE'S FOR YOU

MONDAY MORNING PEP TALKS

234

THIS ONE'S FOR YOU

This post is for you! It's always for you!

This is to remind you that you're pretty amazing, because you may, in the course of the week, have forgotten it.

This is to remind you that you are more than enough, but never stop learning!

This is to remind you that you may have a bad day, but you have an amazing life. Look at everything that's around you! Look at the breath your breathing, it's amazing, right?

This is to remind you that you are stronger than you ever give yourself credit for! You can move mountains if you want to, you just have to want it bad enough! You have to be willing to know that

your mountain might take form in different ways, but you have the strength to move them.

This is to remind you that there is beauty and miracles and love surrounding you all day. You just have to be willing to see them. You have to be able to see it in all the small and mundaneness of everyday life.

This is to remind you that you shouldn't worry too much about the little things that stress you out. It's not worth the sleep you'll lose, or the stress you'll feel. Let it go! You have bigger fish to fry!

This is to remind you that the universe is ALWAYS on your side. ALWAYS! Not just on good days, but on the not so good days too, when it's showing us, teaching us, growing us for greater things.

This is to remind you that you are so important to the world regardless of what you do. The world needs you, and all the personality, talents, and charm you bring to the lives of those you reach and beyond.

This is to remind you that you should take some time to just enjoy you! You're worth it!

This is to remind you that forgiveness is your path to freedom. Forgive as often as necessary. Forgive for yourself, not for anyone else. Forgive, because you know whoever hurt you was probably hurting, and it probably had very little to do with you. Forgive, because you can.

This is to remind you fun is not a bad word!
Laughter is medicine. Friendships should be
cherished. Family is key!

This is to remind you that you should make time
for the people and things that are important to you.
Everything else can wait.

This is to remind you that success is not always
how much money you make, or what your job title
says, but true success is the legacy you leave long
after you're gone.

This is to remind you of the power of love! Love for
yourself, love for others. Love liberally!

This is to remind you to take a break! You don't
have to do it albeit all, know it all. Sometimes, you
just need to rest, and repower!

This is to remind you that your thoughts impact
your actions, so make them good!

This is to remind you that you should always speak
your truth, but do so in a respectful way. Even if
it's hard. Even if you get nervous, speak it out,
share your truth.

This is to remind you that you are a light in the
world, let it shine!

This is to remind you that you are responsible for
the energy you bring into a room, raise it higher!

This is to remind you that you, yes you, are capable of living a life beyond your wildest dreams!

This is for you, because you may have needed to hear this this week, or maybe next, regardless, it's always true!

Here's to you, and all you do!

With Appreciation---

Colene

FIND THE
MIRACLES

MONDAY MORNING PEP TALKS

FIND THE MIRACLES

note: this is still the piece that I've written that I'm the most proud of, and has received the most feedback.)

Last week was tough. I mean physically and emotionally tough. It was one of those weeks that caused me to flex every ounce of heart and love I had in my possession, and it still didn't seem like enough. On Monday morning my dear friend Andrea's father had a massive stroke. It was obviously unexpected as most strokes are, and we did not know how things were going to end. Through the course of the day, there were text messages back and forth between myself and her, and myself and another friend who was there at the hospital with her. During the day, we got word that he may not recover from the damage he suffered from the stroke. After work, I went and sat at the hospital with her and her mother to help keep them company. It was an odd feeling,

knowing that someone's life could change so quickly.

I went home that night and I prayed. I prayed for Andrea. I prayed for her mother. I prayed for her family. I prayed that God would heal her father. I prayed for a miracle. I prayed. It was the only thing I could think of to do that might make a difference.

Tuesday, the report was the same. Andrea and her mother were still at the hospital. I went back up after work, and sat and told stories. I saw family members and friends come in and out. I saw students whose lives had been changed by the role her father played in their lives. I saw the effect one person can have on so many lives. It was inspiring. Afterwards, I went home and prayed again.

On Wednesday, one of my best friends found out she was having a girl! I was THRILLED as we have had multiple conversations regarding the sex of her child. I knew it was a girl, I called it the second she told me she was pregnant. We talked about how it now all feels real that she's actually having a baby. We talked about the future with prom dresses, wedding dresses and shaving legs! We laughed! I cried from joy! I went home and prayed again. I prayed for the little girl that is growing inside Katie. I prayed for Andrea. I prayed, still hoping for a miracle.

What I didn't realize then was that God was showing me miracles, just not in the form I expected. We always talk about birth being a

miracle, and it totally is, but in the reverse, we should start to see the miracle that is death.

What I witnessed this week was nothing short of miraculous. I saw the depths of friendship stretched to points none of us knew existed. I saw that having great friends allows you to be a great friend. I saw people put their lives on hold to help. I saw a friend start to believe in something bigger than himself again. I came to realize that every step of my journey, the good, the bad, lead me to be here, in Kentucky, to be a friend to my friends in need, in babies and in death. I honestly stood in awe of the beauty of friendship. And that WAS the miracle.

All of these people come from different places. Most of us did not grow up together, but yet, in the most perfect way, we all met, and became friends. It amazes me that out of all the people in the world, that I have the friends that I do. We all met because we all have something that we need to provide to each other. We all have something that we need to gain from each other. We all need each other. Coming to that understanding puts me at peace. It makes me understand that there is beauty in life and in death. There is beauty in the possibility of a new baby. There is reasoning in friendship. There are miracles around us every single day if we honestly take the time to see them. They may not always appear in a turning water into wine kind of way, but instead in a sense of understanding and growth. I am thankful!

George passed away on Friday. He left a legacy that most of us can only wish we could leave. He was one of those people who truly left the world a better place. He reminds us that we all have an opportunity to make a difference, to leave a legacy, to impact a life.

I spent most of the weekend thinking about what legacy I want to leave, and how I plan to ensure I can impact people in my own way. I continue to pray for my dear friend and her family. Most importantly, I continue to believe in miracles!

Find the miracle---

Colene

JUST
BREATHE

MONDAY MORNING PEP TALKS

JUST BREATHE

A few weeks ago I took my guy on a "field trip" to Mammoth Cave. He's been obsessed with going since I've met him, and has researched more details than any person really needs to know about Mammoth Cave. So we finally had a free weekend to make our way the 2.5 hours to see the cave!

In all of our excitement on the way down there, and even after we got there, I didn't have much time to think about one crucial thing... I hate small spaces! Although I had been to Mammoth Cave before, I had forgotten about the fact that there are some small spaces. This realization didn't hit me until we were with our tour group and our guide, who happened to be a friend of mine, mentioned a part of the cave called "Fat Man's Misery". His words, "there are some parts of the cave that get pretty tight, and low, so be careful. Also, this isn't like King's Island, there are no little doors that

people can come in from, if you get hurt, it may take some time for emergency responders to get to you."

Ummm, What?!? While I appreciate his warning, what I heard was the following, "DANGER, you will be trapped in a small hole in a cave. DANGER, if you get hurt, you will probably die because it may take DAYS for someone to find you! DANGER, you will be eaten by a large bobcat!"

So, I don't even think there are bobcats in the caves, especially not in the sections made for tours, but it just goes to show that your mind is a powerful force. As we entered the cave, and the other guide locked the door, I felt it coming... that dreaded sense of panic and overwhelm and I knew, that more than anything, I had to get it under control as we were about to embark on a 2 hour tour.

As we started walking, my guy, who was lost in his excitement, began talking to the other tour guide, asking questions, and telling him the information that he knew. I, on the other hand, was beginning to sweat and started to feel my heart race. It was a cool 60 degrees in the cave and I was sweating like I was running on a beach. I knew that this could quickly get out of control, if I didn't nip it in the bud soon.

What did I do? I started to reframe the conversation I was having with myself in my head, telling myself that it was safe for me to be in the cave, that hundreds of thousands of people go through the

caves just fine, that I will make it out just fine. I visualized myself coming out of the cave at the end, smiling and happy to make it through. Most importantly, what I did next changed the whole course of the rest of the tour... I began to breathe!

I very consciously inhaled for 10 seconds, held it for 5 seconds, and then exhaled for 10 seconds. Over and over again for the first 10 minutes of the cave tour. The next thing I knew I was in an open space, and was fine.

The rest of the tour was a ball! We had a great time, and met a really nice family that walked near us during most of the tour. By the end, I was sad that it was over, and promised my guy we could come back soon to take a different tour.

Why am I telling you about my near panic attack?

The steps I took to release the panic, and overwhelm are steps you can take in your everyday life. The second before you feel overwhelmed (you can always feel it coming up), STOP and start to reframe the situation. Then, begin to consciously breathe. The rhythm I gave earlier works best:
Inhale for 10 seconds
Hold for 5 seconds
Exhale for 10 seconds
Repeat

Moving myself to the present moment through breathing and reframing, allowed me the

opportunity to really enjoy the experience of Mammoth Cave, and spending time with my guy.

Try it out for yourself, let me know how it works!

In the words of Faith Hill, "Just Breathe"!

Love,

Colene

ABOUT THE AUTHOR

Colene Elridge is a coach, speaker, writer and friend! She's passionate about two things, creating better work, and creating better lives. She's a sought after speaker and trainer, known for bringing realness and sense of humor to everything she does. But, it's not all fun and games, she knows her stuff! She spent nearly 15 years in human resources and gets both the strategy and practicability of work. She's been featured in both print and video media as an expert in her field. Colene loves to show people the power of their possibilities, and how we can all BE MORE than our circumstances. Colene can be found, usually with sweet tea in her hand and laughter in her heart!

Made in the USA
San Bernardino, CA
17 November 2018